CULTURAL TRADITIONS IN
NORTHERN IRELAND

VARIETIES OF SCOTTISHNESS

Previous conferences in this series have included:

Varieties of Irishness, 1989
Varieties of Britishness, 1990
All Europeans Now? 1991

Cultural Traditions in Northern Ireland

Varieties of Scottishness

Exploring the Ulster-Scottish Connection

Proceedings of the Cultural Traditions Group Conference
March 1996

Edited by John Erskine and Gordon Lucy

The Institute of Irish Studies
The Queen's University of Belfast
1997

First published 1997
The Institute of Irish Studies
The Queen's University of Belfast

This book has received support from the Cultural Traditions Programme of the Community Relations Council which aims to encourage acceptance of cultural diversity.

British Library Cataloguing in Publication Data.
A catalogue record for this book is available from the British Library.

ISBN 0 85389 668 2

Cover design and typesetting by W. & G. Baird Ltd

Typeset in Baskerville

Printed by W. & G. Baird Ltd, Antrim, Northern Ireland

CONTENTS

Dunluce Castle, from a nineteenth-century engraving by W. H. Bartlett, a symbol
and reminder of the historic links between Ulster and the west of Scotland.

ACKNOWLEDGEMENTS

Very many people were involved in the organization and realization of the 'Varieties of Scottishness' conference in March 1996. It would be remiss of the conference steering group not to take this opportunity to record its thanks and indebtedness to the many people who contributed to the making and success of the conference: to the Cultural Traditions Group which sponsored the conference; to the Community Relations Council which initiated and encouraged the project (and in particular to Dr Maurna Crozier and Mark Adair); to the Director, Trustees and staff of the Ulster Museum who provided accommodation and willing assistance; to the Vice-Chancellor and staff of the Queen's University who provided hospitality; to Dr Ronnie Buchanan who chaired the conference; to Dr John Dunlop, Dr Cahal Dallat and Dr Philip Robinson who chaired the three major sessions; to the speakers who provided the papers and who responded so enthusiastically to the invitation to speak; and, not least, to the great number of people who attended the conference and whose presence justified the whole undertaking. Lastly, the members of the steering group must record their thanks to the conference secretary, Gordon Smith, for his hard work and his reassuring presence: only they know what he achieved.

* * * * * *

The editors would also like to express their thanks to all those who have contributed so generously and in so many ways to the production of this book: to the writers for their assistance in preparing and editing the text; to Dr Roger Strong of the Public Record Office of Northern Ireland; to Dr Vivienne Pollock and Pat McLean of the Ulster Museum; to Tom Watson of Belfast Public Library; to John Killen of the Linen Hall Library; to Deborah Hunter and Susanna Kerr of the National Galleries of Scotland; to Fiona Murray and Stella MacDermott of the Community Relations Council; to Carolyn Muncaster for preparing the index; the audio-visual department of the Queen's University, to many others for their various assistance; and not least to Margaret McNulty of the Institute of Irish Studies who steered the whole undertaking to completion.

CONTRIBUTORS

Ivan Herbison is a Lecturer in the Department of English at the Queen's University of Belfast. A specialist in Anglo-Saxon and Old English, he has also written widely on the traditions of the Rhyming Weavers, and notably on his forbear, David Herbison. He is the author of *Webs of Fancy: Poems of David Herbison, the Bard of Dunclug* (1980) and *Language, Literature and Cultural Identity: an Ulster-Scots Perspective* (1989).

Edith M. Johnston-Liik was formerly Professor of History at Macquarie University, Sydney. She is the author of *Great Britain and Ireland, 1760-1800* (1963) and *Ireland in the Eighteenth Century* (1974). She is currently an Honorary Senior Research Fellow at the Queen's University of Belfast and Director of the History of the Parliament of Ireland project.

Billy Kay is a writer, lecturer, and award-winning broadcaster of radio and television programmes with a special interest in the relationship between his native Scotland and Ulster. His programmes have included 'From the Gorbals to Gweedore' in the *Odyssey* series and 'The Scots of Ulster'. He also has a particular interest in the history and use of the Scots language and is the author of *Scots: the Mither Tongue* (2nd ed. 1993).

David N. Livingstone is Professor of Geography at the Queen's University of Belfast and a Fellow of the British Academy. He has written widely on the history of geography, the historical geography of science, and the relationship between science and religion. He is the author of *Nathaniel Southgate Shaler and the Culture of American Science* (1987), *Darwin's Forgotten Defenders* (1987) and the *The Geographical Tradition* (1992).

Linde Lunney has researched and published on the literature, culture and language of eighteenth- and early nineteenth-century Ulster and has written on aspects of the linguistic and cultural relations between Ulster and Scotland. She is currently Editorial Secretary of the Dictionary of Irish Biography project based at the Royal Irish Academy in Dublin.

Elaine McFarland is a Senior Lecturer at Glagow Caledonian University and subject leader in History. She is the author of *Protestants First! Orangeism in Nineteenth-Century Scotland* (1990) and *Ireland and Scotland in the Age of Revolution* (1994) a study of Ulster-Scottish political connections in the last decade of the eighteenth century. Her current project is a study of the Irish Home Ruler, John Ferguson.

Graham Walker is a Reader in the Department of Politics at the Queen's University of Belfast. He is the author of *The Politics of Frustration: Harry Midgley and the Failure of Labour* (1986), *Thomas Johnston* (1988) and *Intimate Strangers: Political and Cultural Interaction between Scotland and Ulster in Modern Times* (1995). He is co-editor of *Sermons and Battle Hymns: Protestant Popular Culture in Modern Scotland* (1990) and *Unionism in Modern Ireland: New Perspectives on Politics and Culture* (1996).

. . . the connection between West Scotland and North-East Ireland is a constant factor in history.

G. M. Trevelyan

. . . but individual authors are still too bound by national horizons to consider the western littoral . . . or to take Down and Antrim along with south-west Scotland as a unit for investigation. But such are the ties of geography and culture that it could not fail to be exciting if we took such bold steps next.

T. C. Smout

INTRODUCTION

A constant factor

At their closest point, some twelve miles of water separate the coasts of Ulster and Scotland. Yet, perhaps 'separate' is not in fact the most appropriate word to use. Indeed, to talk of this stretch of water 'separating' the two places is in itself to betray a very modern point of view for until comparatively recently water was regarded as much as a means of communication as an obstacle to it. From the earliest times to the present – from Mesolithic settler and missionary saint to migrant seasonal labourer and twentieth-century medical student – the narrow waters of the North Channel have witnessed and carried a constant traffic of people and ideas between the two coasts. Proinsias MacCana has remarked: 'Archaeologists speak of an "Irish Sea culture-province" . . . ; one might with comparable justification speak of a North Channel culture-province within which obtained a free currency of ideas – literary, intellectual and artistic.'

Indeed, while the concept of water as thoroughfare rather than obstacle may come as surprise to many living in the very different circumstances of the last decade of the second millennium – when the North Channel appears to be simply an irritating and expensive interruption to the journey of the business traveller, the student or the holidaymaker – it is no new concept to the archaeologist or the historian of the early period. Sea-borne influence and sea-borne power, based in and around the North Channel – from the Clyde-Carlingford cairns to the Lordship of the Isles and the MacDonald hegemony – are well-attested phenomena. Inevitably, therefore, the very proximity of these two coastlines, the one visible daily from the other, has had a profound and enduring influence in shaping the experience and history of both places. Thus, instead of talking of separation it might be equally accurate to observe that the very narrowness of the North Channel has acted as a link rather than as a barrier between Ulster and Scotland.

Varieties of Scottishness

While most people instinctively recognise that there is a close, historical relationship between Ulster and Scotland, not many could discuss the significance and complexity of that relationship in any detail.
This is hardly surprising, however, for until recently the nature,
extent and influence of that relationship have been the subject of
only a handful of systematic studies. As a consequence, much of the
recent cultural debate in Northern Ireland has been confined to an
often debilitatingly insular framework and has failed to include a
complementary examination of the importance of inter-insular
influence. Indeed, the limitations of such an insular approach were
recognised at the first of the 'Varieties' conferences, when Michael
Longley drew attention to the inhibiting tendency to 'ignore the
Scottish horizon'.

It was, therefore, in order to broaden the cultural discussion and
to embark upon an initial exploration of the Scottish horizon, that
the Cultural Traditions Group organised its 'Varieties of Scottishness'
conference in the spring of 1996. The conference, which was held at
the Ulster Museum and the Queen's University on 1 and 2 March, set
out to investigate something of the nature of the Ulster-Scottish connection and to explore the relationship between the two places. The
seven papers published in this volume represent the major contributions to that conference.

The organization of the conference was delegated to a steering
group of the Cultural Traditions Group which was convened for the
purpose. Almost inevitably, the most difficult problem facing the
steering group was to decide not so much what to include as what to
leave out. It simply was not possible to cover every aspect of centuries
of Ulidio-Scottish interaction in a single day. So, in the end and after
much discussion, it was decided to concentrate on the last three centuries and to investigate the connections between Ulster and
Scotland through three broad themes: *Religion, Education and Ideas*;
History and Politics; and *Language and Literature*. These three themes
in themselves clearly do not represent the totality of this Ulidio-
Scottish example of what has been called 'cultural transfretation' –
that is, the constant interplay of cultural influence across a narrow
stretch of water. Furthermore, it was not possible to treat each theme
exhaustively – for each merited a conference in its own right – nor
was it possible to examine other, related topics such as migration,
trade, commerce, industry, agriculture, transport, sport, music or
folk culture. However, despite these limitations, it was hoped that the

three themes which were selected would offer the speakers sufficient opportunity for both scope and depth. Happily, this seems to have been the case, for the members of the steering group were greatly encouraged not only by the enthusiasm with which the speakers responded to the whole project but also by the diversity of subject and approach evident in their papers.

The conference was opened by Billy Kay who was faced with the daunting task of drawing together the many threads of the Ulster-Scottish connection in his wide-ranging keynote address. In the session on *Religion, Education and Ideas*, E.M. Johnston-Liik identified the major religious and intellectual developments in the Ulster-Scottish connection during the eighteenth century, while David Livingstone examined a particular instance of divergence in religious responses to science in nineteenth-century Ulster and Scotland. In their examination of *History and Politics*, Elaine McFarland traced the intense political interaction between Scotland and Ulster in the last decade of the eighteenth century, while Graham Walker studied developments and change in the political relations between the two places over the past one hundred years. Finally, under the heading of *Language and Literature*, Linde Lunney considered language and identity within the Ulster-Scots community, while Ivan Herbison investigated the significance and the demise of the Ulster-Scots literary tradition.

A broader horizon?

Many themes and motifs, which it falls outside the scope of this introduction to discuss in full, recurred in the various papers and linked the different sessions. However, mention should perhaps be made of one figure who did emerge in a majority of papers and who perhaps provided something of a focus for the conference as a whole: Francis Hutcheson. Of Scottish ancestry, an Ulsterman by birth, a teacher in a Dublin academy, and Professor of Moral Philosophy at the University of Glasgow in the second quarter of the eighteenth century, Hutcheson's real significance has only recently become more fully recognized outside those university departments of philosophy of which he was once the preserve. Hutcheson's philosophy informed the religious, moral and political thinking of his day and of his century – in Scotland, Ulster and America – so much so that he became known as the 'Father' of the Scottish Enlightenment.

The significance of Hutcheson's thinking was only one of the many topics that became the subject of discussion during the questions and conversations which followed the papers. Furthermore, it soon became clear that many of those present felt that, in order to build on the work of the conference papers, there was an urgent need for further, more widespread investigation of the Ulster-Scottish connection at academic level. Several suggestions were made: among them, that the conference should itself become a regular event but also, and more importantly, that some structure or structures should be established within the university sector to facilitate the development of the study of Ulster-Scottish history, influence and interaction.

Given the thorough and fascinating beginning made by the conference and the clear demonstration that Ulster-Scottish studies have an informed, popular audience as well as a firm, academic basis, it is certainly to be hoped that both the conference and this book will indeed stimulate further interest, research and reflection. Since Ulster-Scottish studies, in all their diversity, are not the preserve of any one tradition and since they relate to both Ulster *and* Scotland, it may not be too much to suggest that there is at least a case for the bilateral – indeed, bilittoral – establishment of an inter-university centre, school or institute for the multi-disciplinary development of Ulster-Scottish studies.

Such an institution could indeed achieve much for, whether such a body comes into existence or not, it is clear that there is much work to be done. And it is surely in the common interest and to the mutual benefit of all of those who live on either side of the North Channel to understand themselves, and each other, better.

John Erskine
Gordon Lucy

KEYNOTE ADDRESS

SHAMROCK AND THISTLE ENTWINED

Billy Kay

> I love my native land, no doubt,
>   Attach'd to her thro' thick and thin;
> Yet tho' I'm *Irish* all *without*,
> I'm every item *Scotch within.*[1]

In these words Samuel Thomson, a poet of the nineteenth century, sums up the strong sense of dual nationality felt by Ulster-Scots. Now, many people of Scots descent furth of Scotland feel a nostalgic tie to the 'auld country'; but in Ulster the roots go a lot deeper and have been nourished over the centuries by the close proximity and consequent cultural interchange between Scotland and the north of Ireland. When the Galloway coast is not shrouded in mist, the green hills of Antrim can be seen shimmering across the water. With only twelve miles of sea separating us, it is little wonder that influences across the sheuch, as the North Channel is referred to colloquially, should be both profound and permanent.

Most historians now agree that Ireland's first inhabitants crossed from Scotland by this route in the Early Mesolithic period. It was the Celtic tribe, the Scotti, crossing from Ulster to Argyll – the coast of the Gael – in the fifth and sixth centuries, who gave Scotland her name, her initial experience of Christianity and her Gaelic tongue which survives in those same communities on her western seaboard. Gaelic acted as a *lingua franca* for centuries as the MacDonnell Lords of the Isles held power in a thalassocracy, or sea-going realm, which stretched from the Butt of Lewis to the Isle of Man. Through marriage they also became Lords of Antrim and when their power waned in Scotland, due to encroachment by the Scottish Crown, Antrim naturally became their stronghold, the only problem being the native Irish clans. Thousands of Hebrideans took part in this mid-sixteenth-century military expansion and settlement in the Glens of Antrim. By then it was simply the continuation of an ancient pattern. In the

fourteenth century, when the Scots had fought for their country with
that precocious and ultimately irresistible sense of national identity
against Edward I and Edward II of England, King Robert the Bruce's
brother, Edward, saw Celtic Ulster as a natural cockpit for resisting
English expansion and, no doubt, strengthening Scotland's natural
sphere of influence there.

From the late sixteenth and during the seventeenth century it was
the turn of thousands of lowland, mainly Calvinist, Scots to swarm
across the channel and to move into the political vacuum created by
the destruction of Gaelic Ulster. Their settlement runs in a huge arch
from the Ards peninsula of County Down up through Antrim and
north Derry to taper out in the Laggan region of east Donegal. In
religion, music, literary tradition and especially in its Scots language
it is very much an extension of the western Lowlands of Scotland. Its
heartland covers a major swathe of Ulster and influences every other
part of the province, both in the Republic and Northern Ireland.

The most recent, major manifestation of this cross-channel process
was one which changed the character of the Scottish Lowlands.
There, radical improvement in Scottish agriculture in the late eighteenth century turned the eastern Lowlands into a vast granary of
corn which needed to be harvested quickly by hand. Highland and
Irish harvesters flocked there as seasonal migrants, the latter becoming more and more predominant as cheap regular sailings were introduced in the 1820s. The Scottish newspapers of the period are full of
reports like the following from the *Scottish Guardian* of 24 August
1849:

> The *Londonderry* brought over from Ireland the extraordinary
> number of 1,700 human beings at one trip . . . The poor creatures
> filled every corner from stem to stern, clustering round the bul-
> wark as thick as bees.[2]

Seasonal migration continued with tattie howkers and navvies –
building railways, roads, tunnels and hydro schemes – till the middle of our own century. Thousands settled as permanent work
became available in the textile industry and in the rapidly expanding
iron industry which was based on the Scottish coalfield. By 1851 there
was a settled Irish community in Scotland numbering 200,000
although that figure does not include those children born in
Scotland who would have considered themselves Irish. These people
maintained close links with Donegal, many of their descendants
returning to live there a hundred years after the main migration, with

the upturn in the Irish economy in the 1970s and 1980s. While the majority of the Irish who came were Roman Catholic – and often Gaelic speakers from areas like Glencolumbkille, the Rosses and Gweedore in west Donegal – it is estimated that up to 25% of the migrants were Ulster Protestants, descended no doubt from those Lowlanders of the last major migration in the other direction in the seventeenth century. According to Alan Campbell in his book *The Lanarkshire Miners*, the Irish in Larkhall were:

> 'almost 100% Orange' . . . The Protestant Irish, being originally of Scottish stock and sharing a common religion, were much less alien than the Catholic immigrants. Robert Smillie, a Protestant immigrant to Larkhall from Belfast, recalled that his grandmother could recite ballads in Scots Doric, even though she had lived in Ireland all her life, and he himself had read Burns as a boy.[3]

It is perhaps no coincidence that those places where sectarian bigotry exists in Scotland today were industrial flashpoints in the late nineteenth century. With native colliers struggling to maintain conditions, coalmasters exploited the ready availability of cheap Irish labour. That, in addition to the importation of the Orange and Green conflict from Ulster, produced a potent brew and a few good tunes in parts of the Scottish coalfield.

As a result of all this interaction, I feel that a strong case can be made for defining the land that stretches from the west coast of Ulster to the east coast of Scotland as one distinctive cultural area. This is a notion with which few politicians would concur but which finds remarkable support in the perception of ordinary people. People from the south of Ireland visiting Donegal for the first time remark on the Scottishness of the speech and of the very style of music played by the brilliant traditional fiddlers of the area, many of whom, like the great Johnny Docherty, worked and travelled in Scotland. This is how a musician from the former folk band *Ossian*, and a son of the Donegal Diaspora, George Jackson, referred to the situation in my radio programme, 'From the Gorbals to Gweedore':

> There always seems to be this amazing traffic every week going back and forth from Donegal . . . To me it just seems . . . like another island off the west coast [of Scotland]. And funnily enough, when we were in Ireland in the summer, at the festival in Ballysadare, there were some people from Kerry in the very south and they were

asking whether I had any Irish connections and I was telling them about Donegal, and they said, 'Oh, they're Scots anyway really', ye know. And they [the Donegal people] were sayin' as well that they had more in common with the Scots than they had with the people down in Kerry and they even said that Donegal was just like an island off the west coast of Scotland.[4]

This perception is reinforced if you know the dialectology of Gaelic. Ulster Gaelic speakers can communicate with Scots Gaels with far greater facility than with those who have the dialects of Irish spoken farther south. Again, if you come from Scots-speaking areas in Ulster you are frequently perceived as originating in Caledonia rather than Hibernia. When I recorded distillery workers from Bushmills for a programme on the history of the language, several spoke of having to convince people they 'were fae the north coast' after being mistaken for natives of Scotland outwith their home areas. John Kennedy – fae Cullybackey, County Antrim, home of a world champion pipe band (that's another story) and the braid Ulster tongue – said:

> We yist tae go tae Portrush every 13th o July wi the baund, an I mind singin a song, an there wes a lady fae Scoatlan cam ower tae me . . . an she says, 'Hey, son, hou lang ur ye ower for?' An I've never been tae Scoatlan in ma life. The All Ireland [traditional singing competition] wes in Kilkenny last year . . . A lady says tae me afterwards, 'I love that song', but she says, 'there were some o the words I couldnae make out . . . ye sound a bit Scotch!' I says, 'I'm blamed for that!'[5]

John Kennedy is of course an important County Antrim tradition-bearer and, like his peers all over the north, carries Scots language, ballads, songs and singing style easily as part of his history and culture. One of John's songs, 'Jeremy's Bridge' is an Antrim variant of what in my native Irvine Valley is sung as 'Derval Dam', with its distinctive chorus:

> Whaur dae ye bide? Whaur dae ye stey?
> Come tell tae me yer name.
> Wad yer faither no be angry nou,
> Gin I wes tae see ye hame?

Countless other Scottish popular songs and rhymes were adapted and

given Ulster settings. In Greyabbey (Greba) 'Wha saw the tattie howkers?' became:

> Wha seen the Greba lasses,
> Wha seen them gang awa,
> Wha seen the Greba lasses,
> Gangan doon the Hard Breid Raw?
>
> Some o thaim had buits an stockins,
> Some o thaim had nane ava,
> Some o thaim had big bare backsides,
> Gangan doon the Hard Breid Raw.[6]

Ayrshire and Antrim, Galloway and Down have been part of a
shared cultural area since at least the seventeenth century. One of the
songs Burns collected, 'Ower the Muir, Amang the Heather', he got
from Jean Glover, a Kilmarnock lassie who travelled the area and
made a living as an entertainer along with her man whom Burns
described as 'a sleight of hand blackguard' or magician. Another son
o auld Killie, a soldier, met up with her in Letterkenny, her final rest-
ing place.

As a Scot committed to Scottish culture, and fascinated by its many
thrawn and diverse manifestations, I cannot stress enough the importance I place on this Scottish dimension in Ulster. Exiles may cele-
brate Rabbie or St Andrew the world over but, with the possible
exception of the diminishing Gaelic enclave in Cape Breton Island, I
would regard Ulster as the only major recognisable Scottish cultural
community outside Scotland. I would like to explore this idea further
with some specific examples.

Language

The marked Lowland Scots strand in the English spoken in the
Gaeltacht of west Donegal, of course, was not just the result of historic
seasonal migration to Scotland. The Irish-speaking tattie howkers
simply had to cross over to the fertile east of their own county to pick
up the same employment and the same language in the solidly Scots-
planted area of the Laggan: 'Goin up till the Lagan tae lift the Scotch'
was the way the workers described the linguistic acquisition available
with the work. One west Donegal harvester addressed a traveller in
his home area thus: 'It's the Irish we speak among wursels, but we hae
eneuch Scotch to speak till yer honer.'[7]

Given the speed with which Scottish colonists have divested themselves of their native tongues elsewhere in the world in more recent
times – a process which has its roots in the colonised mentality of
the Scots since the Union of 1707 – the most remarkable feature of
the Ulster-Scots communities is their retention of Scots in their everyday speech. Many of the areas have not had a fresh influx of Scots settlers for more than three hundred years and have been exposed to
the anglicising 'improvers' as much as any place in Scotland, yet their
Scots is rich, expressive and thrang with words you rarely come across
in Scotland: *ferntickles* (freckles), *gowpinfu* (two handfuls), *forenenst*
(opposite), *wale* (select), and *couter* (ploughhead) are a few of the
words I recorded folk using, all set in a dialect as rich as anything in
my native Ayrshire. The fishing port of Portavogie on the Ards
peninsula is one of the strongholds of Ulster-Scots speech. There I
had the unusual experience of hearing a fellow Scot, a lad from
Glasgow, describe how he had picked up Scots words like *thrawn*
(stubborn), *wheen* (lots of) and *rape* (rope) since he had moved to
Ireland. The Ulster-Scots dialects have long been distinctive and wor-
thy of comment. Writing in the nineteenth century, the Rev. John
Graham described his parishioners in Maghera, County
Londonderry, thus:

> The Dissenters speak broad Scotch, and are in the habit of using
> terms and expressions long since obsolete, even in Scotland, and
> which are only to be found in the glossary annexed to the bishop
> of Dunkeld's translation of Virgil.[8]

Literature

The reference to the Bishop of Dunkeld, Gavin Douglas (c.1474-
1522), in relation to the parishioners' language is apt, considering
the Ulster folk's love of literature in the auld leid. Throughout the
eighteenth century, editions of earlier Scots literature – Barbour's
Brus, Blin Harry's *Wallace*, and the poetry of Sir David Lyndsay and
Alexander Montgomerie – were available in chapbook form or in
Belfast editions. When the new Scots poetry of the eighteenth-century vernacular revival reached Ulster it was not only a huge popular
success – children could recite whole sections of Ramsay's *Gentle
Shepherd* – but sparked off a vibrant Ulster-Scots poetic revival.
Francis Boyle, from County Down, was born around 1730, so in using
his local Scots vernacular he is part of a tradition that was established

before the poetry of Burns took the Scottish world by storm. Here is part of his poem, 'The Author's Address to his Old Gelding':

> Thy bonny face wi' star an' snip,
> Thy sleekit hide, thy weel turn't hip;
> Thy tail, or mane, I winnae clip,
>   Or poll thee bare;
> Like them that gang on board a ship
>   For Glasgow fair.
>
> When snaws lie lang, an' frost is keen
> An' neither grass nor foliage seen,
> I gather whins that's young an' green
>   An' them prepare,
> An' feed thee wi' them morn an' e'en
>   To sleek thy hair.[9]

The spark already kindled became a conflagration when in 1787, the same year as the first Edinburgh edition, the works of Burns were published in Belfast. Samuel Thomson of Carngranny, County Antrim, wrote:

> Tho' Allan Ramsay blythly ranted,
> An' tun'd his reed wi' merry glee;
>   Yet faith that *something* ay he wanted,
> That makes my Burns sae dear to me.[10]

Thomson was one of at least seven Ulster poets who made the pilgrimage to Scotland to visit the genius in his Ayrshire lair. Burns would have been delighted with the quality of the writing of many of the Ulster poets. In 'The Irish Cottier's Death and Burial', for example, James Orr of Ballycarry uses Burns's 'The Cottar's Saturday Night' as a model, but rarely falls into the artificial posturing in the stilted passages in Burns's poem. Orr's poem is better for its simple naturalism:

> Wi' patient watchfu'ness, lasses an' lads,
>   Carefu' an' kin', surroun' his clean caff bed,
> Ane to his lips the coolin' cordial ha'ds,
>   An' ane behin' supports his achin' head;
>   Some bin' the arm that lately has been bled,

The Sire turns o'er, with patriarchal grace
The big ha-Bible, ance his Father's pride.

An illustration from a late nineteenth-century edition of Burns' *The Cottar's Saturday Night* published by the Belfast firm of Marcus Ward.

In my childhood [in County Down] I was fortunate enough to live for several years in the household of a small farmer, Alexander Gaw . . . Apart from the Bible . . . I can remember only three other books in which Alexander Gaw showed any interest. They were Emerson's Essays, *A Serious Call to a Devout and Holy Life* by William Law, and Robert Burns' Poems; and the only pages of the poet unthumbed was the glossary.

Sam Hanna Bell in *Erin's Orange Lily*

> An' some burn bricks his feet mair warm to mak;
>   If e'er he doze, how noiselessly they tread!
> An' stap the lights to mak the bield be black,
> An' aft the bedside lea, an' aft slip saftly back.[11]

The strength of identity with the language and Scots tradition was such that it travelled with the Ulster colonists who became the Scotch-Irish ethnic group predominant in Pennsylvania, Appalachia and many areas of the American South. On the Pennsylvania frontier, at the time of the Whiskey Rebellion, there took place a flyting – Scots for a poetic rammy – between Ulster-born David Bruce and Kintyre-born Hugh Henry Brackenridge. This is Bruce on the drink at the centre of local politics in 1794:

> Great Pow'r, that warms the heart and liver,
> And puts the bluid a' in a fever,
> If dull and heartless I am ever,
>   A blast o' thee
> Maks me as blyth, and brisk, and clever
>   As ony bee.[12]

In an article on the two poets, Claude M. Newlin writes:

> Since Bruce was an ardent Federalist, it is not probable that his Scots verses on political topics were written in dialect for merely sentimental reasons. He no doubt considered Scots to be the most effective medium in which he could appeal to his frontier audience.[13]

This Scots tradition in literature is still engrained in the character of east-Ulster writing today, with poets such as John Clifford, Oonagh McClean and the comic performance verse of the late lamented Alec McAllister providing an unbroken link with the revival of the eighteenth century. This is Alec reflecting on 'Love'.

> Were ye ever in love? Well it's funny to feel,
> You are no to say bad, and you're no very weel;
> Ye hae wild funny feelins up roon by your chest,
> An your heid be's all wandered, like turkeys in mist.
> If you never were you neednae care
> For I was yince an I want nae mair.

On a different literary plane, the novels of the late Sam Hanna Bell are also graced with a native felicity in the use of Scots vernacular. Born in Glasgow, Bell moved back to the County Down home of his maternal grandmother when he was a child, and lived there the rest of his life. I still recall Sam's face lighting up when he told me the story of a Ballymena man discussing the birth of a neighbouring Englishman's son. 'Whit are ye gaun tae cry him?' said the Ballymena man. 'Well, we were thinking of calling him Nathan,' replied the Englishman. 'Get awa oot o that,' said the Ballymena man, 'ye'll hae tae cry him somethin!'

Intellectual links

If Sam Hanna Bell is an example of a Scot who came this way and contributed mightily to Ulster literature, 'the never to be forgotten Hutcheson', as Adam Smith described Francis Hutcheson, is one of many who went the other way and contributed hugely to Scottish intellectual life in the *Blütezeit* of the Scottish Enlightenment of the eighteenth century. Professor of Moral Philosophy at Glasgow – and the first man, incidentally, to teach in the vernacular – Hutcheson went against the hard line Calvinist notion that human nature was inherently corrupt and that faith alone was paramount in the eyes of God. He emphasised the primacy of benevolent human feeling and our ability to respond intuitively to the moral beauty in human nature. He led the way for the rise of the moderate New Licht wing in the Kirk. Burns's satire of an Auld Licht ayatolla/elder in the poem 'Holy Willie's Prayer' could not have been written if Hutcheson had not created the climate in which fundamentalist zealots could be reproached. Hutcheson was born in 1694, the son of a Presbyterian minister in County Down and grandson of a minister who had come over from Ayrshire. His grandfather must have been among the earliest, for the first Presbyterian minister in Ulster ministered to an established flock in Ballycarry in 1611. In 1683 a visitor wrote of the parish: 'the inhabitants all Scotch, not one Irishman nor papist, all Presbiterians except the parson and the clark, who I think is his son'.[14] Hutcheson's brilliance, admired by Adam Smith and David Hume, gives the lie to the modern myth that the Presbyterian inheritance is one of stifling, life-denying conservatism. Historically, Presbyterianism in Ireland has been a leading force for intellectual questioning and radical political reform. Until the mid-nineteenth century all of Ulster's ministers and the vast majority of her

Presbyterian students studied at Scottish universities. As far as the rest of the population was concerned, the precocious Reformation desire for basic mass literacy, spurred on by the necessity to read the word of God, gave the Ulster-Scots communities by far the highest literacy figures in Ireland.

In the later eighteenth century, educated hand-loom weavers were imbued with ideals of freedom and democracy inspired by the American and French revolutions and expressed in the works of Thomas Paine. Their radicalism was of course heightened by the discrimination suffered by Presbyterians in Ireland. Presbyterian frustration in Belfast led to the founding of the Society of United Irishmen, a movement which urged Presbyterians and Catholics to unite and overthrow the Anglican Protestant Ascendancy in a reformed, independent, republican Ireland. At the forefront was William Drennan, the son of a New Light minister who had belonged to Francis Hutcheson's coterie in Ulster. Poets like Orr, and Campbell of Ballynure, ministers like the Rev. Adam Hill, and romantic leaders such as Wolfe Tone and Henry Joy McCracken all took arms against the government. The United Irishmen also spawned a similar organisation called the United Scotsmen in the weaving districts of Scotland. It was not simply a copycat organisation, for the old personal links and patterns of migration were constantly renewing themselves:

> The United Scotsmen received considerable support from the Irish . . . Heavy Irish immigration was reported in the late 1790s and it was known that many of these newcomers who took up the weaving profession had prior links with the United Irishmen.[15]

McCracken would have been delighted to see his brethren across the channel join the struggle. A poem, partly attributed to him, called 'The Social Thistle and Shamrock' contains the lines:

> The Scotch and Irish friendly are,
> Their wishes are the same,
> The English nation envy us
> And over us would reign.
> Our historians and our poets
> They always did maintain
> That the origin of Scottishmen
> And Irish are the same . . .

And to conclude and end my song,
May we live long to see
The thistle and the shamrock
Entwine the olive tree.[16]

Politics and diversity

In the ill-planned insurrection of 1798, many were killed in battle,
hanged for treason, or fled to America. There, their 'settler radicalism'
was in the vanguard of the American Revolution. Many see the defeat
of the United Irishmen as the death knell of Presbyterian radicalism in
Ulster, and it would be convenient for the stereotype if it was. But at the
height of anti-Home Rule activity in Ulster in 1912, when Carson and
Craig were recalling the spirit of resistance of the persecuted fore-
fathers of the Ulster-Scot and exhorting true Ulstermen to sign their
Covenant, another Covenant was being organised by the Rev. J.B.
Armour in Ballymoney in the heart of Scotch Antrim. It was *for* Irish
Home Rule, and was signed by over four hundred local Presbyterians.
The very word 'Covenant' – recalling the martyrdom of the founders
of the Kirk in the seventeenth century – could have echoes only in a
Scottish community. Significantly, political opponents claim the man-
tle of being true heirs to the Covenanting tradition. By the end of the
nineteenth century the conservative unionist majority among the
Presbyterians certainly regarded themselves as the descendants of the
Covenanters and missionaries in a land of infidels forbye. In an article
entitled 'The Place and Work of the Presbyterian Church in Ireland',
written in 1890, the Rev. R.J. Lynd cites 'indolence, thriftlessness and
intemperance' as being characteristics of the native Irish. The
Presbyterians, on the other hand, have 'set an example of persistent
and successful industry' which has been 'a blessing to the land'. Lazy
Presbyterians who enjoy a dram do not figure in Lynd's world picture.
Lynd's Presbyterians are all God's chosen children:

> It is God who has planted our Presbyterian Church in Ireland, and
> made this country our Fatherland . . . We are here to do what none
> but ourselves can. Others may be called to equally important work,
> but none can exactly fill the square which has been chiselled for us.[17]

From this you can see that some of the warped ideas of an Ulster
Herrenvolk have their origin in certain sections of the community's
spiritual leadership. Lord Rosebery's famous paean of praise to the
Ulster-Scots endorses the separate race theme:

They are I believe, without exception the toughest, the most dominant, the most irresistible race that exists in the universe at this moment.[18]

The racial dimension, of course, was paralleled on the Roman Catholic side. The father of modern Irish nationalism, Daniel O'Connell, gave the stamp of approval to this limiting and exclusive vision of Irish nationhood when he described Protestants as 'foreign to us since they are of a different religion'.[19] This simplification of history into race and religion is inherently false. In the Catholic/nationalist version of history, for example, the Catholics of the Glens of Antrim are Irish, and belong to the ancient Celtic civilisation of the nation; the Protestants of the rest of Antrim are 'Saxon' interlopers who drove the native Irish off their lands. In fact, the only area where the native Irish were driven out by force of arms was in the Glens – by the Catholic Highlanders of the MacDonnell Lords of the Isles. The Glens were a Scottish Gaelic stronghold until comparatively recently and still maintain strong links with Islay and Kintyre, proving that blood ties and a common history can overcome religious differences. There is no more Calvinist part of Scotland than the Free Kirk-dominated isles of the Hebrides; yet, when I interviewed a lady from there about her sense of identity, her Gaelic culture came first and, outwith Harris, the place she felt most at home was in the Gaeltachti of Donegal. The remnant of Scottish Gaelic culture in the Glens of Antrim was beautifully articulated by Jack McCann in my radio series *The Scots of Ulster*. Said Jack:

If there is such a thing as a ghost in Cushendall, he's standing on the strand there on Christmas morning, *caman* in hand, gazing longingly to the coast of Kintyre in the hope that someone will come and play shinty with him![20]

The people of the Glens are as Scottish as the Scots-speaking Lowlanders; it is their Catholicism which welcomes them into the 'Irish' fold and excludes the others. The twin tramlines of British/Protestant and Irish/Catholic in the politically determined mindsets of the north of Ireland today have meant, of course, that the crucial Scottish dimension has been squeezed out and marginalised in many people's sense of identity.
    The other fact which blows the racial version of Ulster history apart is that of people changing religion to fit in with whichever power

structure prevailed locally. Thus you have Ulster surnames which are
regarded as Protestant yet are obviously of native Irish, and presumably Catholic, origin. Less frequently, you also have people changing
their names – for example, 'O'Boyle' Scotticised to 'Boal' – for the
same reason. The Scottish parallels are obvious. My maternal grandmother was a Donaldson whose family centuries before would have
been Gaelic MacDonalds. All over the Highlands there are name
changelings, usually known only to oral tradition-bearers. I have
heard of 'Boll of Meal Frasers' and 'Dog shit Campbells', and if you
think changing your name or religion for personal gain is ignoble,
consider for a second the motivation of the *Domhnaillaich Tòn
A'Bhotuil* ('Bottle-erse' MacDonalds) from North Uist, so-called
MacDonalds who changed their name for a bottle of whisky,
allegedly![21]

In the frontier territory of Fermanagh and Tyrone yet another
example of the diversity within the term 'Ulster-Scot' can be found:
Border riding families, such as Elliott, Armstrong, Maxwell and
Johnston. When James VI united the Scottish and English Crowns, the
last thing he needed on his now peaceful 'middle shires' were the fighting men whose way of life revolved around cattle reiving, protection
rackets, violence and, in their favour, a lot of good ballads. They were
'encouraged' to leave and join the Scots mercenary forces of Sweden,
Denmark, Prussia, Poland and Russia or to go and hold the outposts of
the Plantation in the debatable lands of Ulster. I can assure you that
religion had never ranked highly as an issue among them. A seventeenth-century English traveller in Liddesdale was astonished by the
lack of places of worship. 'Are there no Christians here?' he enquired.
'Na,' was the reply. 'We's a' Elliots an Armstrangs'.[22]

On that other disputed border, the war of attrition practised by the
IRA during the recent Troubles has had the effect of some farmers
selling up and retreating into 'safer' areas like Antrim, and Down.
Some have actually returned to Galloway and Ayrshire. What they
find if they settle in Wigtownshire is an area with a strong Ulster-
sounding dialect. In the neighbouring Stewartry, the locals speak of
going 'over the Cree and into the Irish' and refer to the inhabitants
of Wigtownshire as 'sowl boys'. As to which side of the 'sheuch'
influenced the other first, it is impossible to tell. This recent migration is smaller than previous ones, but it could gain momentum, God
forbid, if there were dramatic changes for the worse in Northern
Ireland. One weary old gentleman I interviewed living close to the
border on land held by his family since the early seventeenth century

confessed that Scotland would be the choice of the majority of his tradition, should the need arise:

> That's where I would go. And do you know, I've visited Scotland and I've stood on the boat and I've said to the boys that was standing on the boat beside me, 'What made us leave this country? I feel I'm going home.'

A wider perspective

This historic special relationship is valued by both traditions in Ulster, and was respected even by the men of violence. It has had surprising ramifications down through the centuries, even at times of extreme political tension. In the recent Troubles, for example, the IRA has left Scotland out of its bombing campaigns in Britain, a parallel to the situation at the start of the 1641 Rebellion against the Planters, when:

> . . . the Rebels made open proclamations, upon pain of death, that no Scotchman should be stirred in body, goods or lands, and that they should to this purpose write over the lyntels of their doors that they were Scotchmen, and so destruction might pass over their families.[23]

The historian Graham Walker echoed my own experiences in Ulster when he commented that 'as a Scot, both sides presume you are on their side'. What you certainly get is a fellow feeling that, as a Scot, you will understand what is going on in Ulster and sympathise with the people's predicament. Sadly, we sympathise because, of all the links which bind Scotland and Ulster, the only one universally recognised today is the problem of sectarianism in Scottish society. That is a subject blown out of all proportion to its relevance in a Scottish context by the Glasgow-based media's obsession with Rangers and Celtic football clubs. Sectarianism is a sexy subject there because of the glamour surrounding the big teams. Outwith a few historic ghettoes, it would probably have died a death there if it was not for the football dimension. Sectarianism has weakened to such an extent that the bigots and the organisations which encourage bigotry are regarded as an annoying irrelevance by the vast majority of Scots. As I have indicated, it was not always so and there were many violent incidents produced by the clash of cultures in the industrial west of Scotland in the later nineteenth century. The comparatively successful integration of once explosive sections of Scottish society shows that a solution to Ulster's problems is not the absolute impossibility which, until recently, many perceived it to be.

What I have drawn from my work on this Scottish dimension is a wider perspective through which to view my own culture and, I hope, to suggest alternative ways to view the history and culture of my people – Highland and Lowland, Catholic and Protestant – here in Ulster. From this work has emerged the realisation that for centuries the peoples on either side of the narrow sea have interchanged and interacted and migrated back and forward, right through to the present day. As I hope I have shown, we are close cousins divided not by the sheuch, but by politics.

Someone like me, who feels that a new political relationship with England has to emerge if what makes Scotland distinctive as a nation is to survive and thrive, would be called a nationalist. As long as it is recognised that to be international you first have to be national, I would be happy with that definition. Many people here, with the same commitment to their people and the same language and culture, would be happy to be defined as unionist. The majority of Scots of Irish origin consider themselves as belonging to the nationalist tradition in Ireland yet, ironically, along with the tiny, diminishing Conservative and Unionist loyalist vote, they form the staunchest unionist bloc in Scottish politics, a Labour/unionist bloc which so far has been extremely resistant to Scottish nationalist persuasion.

Politically, different experiences have moulded us but, compared to the centuries of shared culture which bind us and which will be revealed in all its depth and diversity at this ground-breaking conference, surely, as the millennium approaches, we can all of us overcome political differences and recognise the celebration of humanity which is at the core of Scottish culture. Being from the Burns country, I err on the optimism of the bard. We are already cousins: how much easier, then, to become brothers and sisters,

> That man tae man the warld ower
> Shall brithers be for aw that.

NOTES

1. Samuel Thomson, 'To Captain M'Dougall, Castle Upton: with a Copy of the Author's Poems' in Ernest Scott and Philip Robinson (eds), *The Country Rhymes of Samuel Thomson, the Bard of Crangranny, 1766-1816* (Bangor: Pretani Press, 1992) p. 62.

2. Quoted in James E. Handley, *The Irish in Modern Scotland* (Cork: Cork University Press, 1947) p. 165.

3. Alan B. Campbell, *The Lanarkshire Miners: a Social History of their Trade Unions, 1775-1974* (Edinburgh: John Donald, 1979) p. 191.

4. Billy Kay (ed.), *Odyssey: Voices from Scotland's Recent Past* (Edinburgh: Polygon, 1980) p. 7. Originally from an interview for the BBC Radio Scotland programme 'From the Gorbals to Gweedore' (1980) in the *Odyssey* series; producer, Billy Kay.

5. Interview with John Kennedy in the BBC Radio Scotland series *The Scots of Ulster* (1989); producer, Michael Shaw; writer and presenter, Billy Kay.

6. See also 'The Greba Lasses', *Ullans*, no. 2, Spring 1994, p. 28.

7. Quoted in John Braidwood, 'Ulster and Elizabethan English' in *Ulster Dialects: an Introductory Symposium* (Holywood: Ulster Folk Museum, 1964) p. 35.

8. Rev. John Graham, 'Parish of Maghera' in W.S. Mason, *A Statistical Account or Parochial Survey of Ireland*, Vol. 1 (Dublin: pr. Graisberry and Campbell, 1814) p. 592.

9. Francis Boyle, 'The Author's Address to his Old Gelding', in his *Miscellaneous Poems*, (Belfast: Lyons, 1811) pp. 43-44.

10. Samuel Thomson, 'Epistle to Mr R[obert] B[urns]' in Scott and Robinson (eds), *The Country Rhymes of Samuel Thomson*, p. 53.

11. James Orr, 'The Irish Cottier's Death and Burial' in Philip Robinson (ed.), *The Country Rhymes of James Orr, the Bard of Ballycarry, 1770-1816* (Bangor: Pretani Press, 1992) p. 29.

12. Claude M. Newlin, 'Dialects on the western Pennsylvania frontier', *American Speech*, vol. 3, 1928, p. 104.

13. ibid., p. 107.

14. Richard Dobbs, 'Description of the county of Antrim' in George Hill (ed.), *An Historical Account of the MacDonnells of Antrim* (Belfast: Archer, 1873) p. 378.

15. Norman Murray, *The Scottish Handloom Weavers, 1790-1850: a Social History* (Edinburgh: John Donald, 1978) p. 212.

16. Henry Joy McCracken, 'The Social Thistle and Shamrock' in R.R. Madden (ed.), *Literary Remains of the United Irishmen of 1798 and Selections from Other Popular Lyrics of their Times...* (Dublin: Duffy, 1887) p. 167ff.

17. R.J. Lynd, 'The place and work of the Presbyterian Church in Ireland' in *Jubilee of the General Assembly of the Presbyterian Church in Ireland, Belfast, July 1890* (Belfast: Witness, 1890) p. 108, p. 106.

18. *The Scotsman*, 2 November 1911, quoted in A. T. Q. Stewart, *The Narrow Ground: Aspects of Ulster, 1609-1969* (London: Faber, 1977) p. 26.

19. Quoted in R.B. McDowell, *Public Opinion and Government in Ireland, 1800-1846* (London: Faber, 1952) p. 124.

20. Interview with Jack McCann in the BBC Radio Scotland series *The Scots of Ulster* (1989); producer, Michael Shaw; writer and presenter, Billy Kay.

21. I am grateful to my co-author of *Knee Deep in Claret*, Cailean Maclean, for access to his family's knowledge of the Gaelic oral and literary traditions.

22. George MacDonald Fraser, *The Steel Bonnets: the Story of the Anglo-Scottish Border Reivers* (London: Barrie and Jenkins, 1971) p. 47. See also Brian Turner, 'An observation on settler names in Fermanagh', *Clogher Record*, vol. 8, 1975, pp. 285-289.

23. Sir Audley Mervyn, quoted in Ian Adamson, *The Identity of Ulster: the Land, the Language and the People* (Bangor: Adamson, 1982) p. 21.

Further reading:

Ian S. Wood (ed.), *Scotland and Ulster* (Edinburgh: Mercat Press, 1994).

Billy Kay, *Scots: the Mither Tongue*, 2nd ed. (Darvel: Alloway, 1993).

Billy Kay and Cailean Maclean, *Knee Deep in Claret* (Skye: Auld Alliance, 1994).

Billy Kay (ed.), *The Complete Odyssey* (Edinburgh: Polygon, 1996).

RELIGION, EDUCATION AND IDEAS

THE DEVELOPMENT OF THE ULSTER-SCOTTISH CONNECTION

E. M. Johnston-Liik

Background

In the brochure and programme for this conference there are two very significant quotations: one by G.M. Trevelyan who remarks that 'the connection between West Scotland and North-East Ireland is a constant factor in history'; and the other by T.C. Smout who writes that:

> . . . individual authors are still too bound by national horizons to consider the western littoral . . . or to take Down and Antrim along with south-west Scotland as a unit for investigation. But such are the ties of geography and culture that it could not fail to be exciting if we took such bold steps next.

It is easy to forget that, before the nineteenth century, land communications were often difficult while sea communications were comparatively easy: hence the great European sea-borne empires of the eighteenth century flourished at the same time as the Irish Bar travelled on horseback from assize to assize. This was particularly true of the area that we are considering. People had gone backwards and forwards over the narrow sea-crossing between Ulster and Scotland from time immemorial so that the appearance of the Scots in the north of Ireland in the sixteenth century was nothing new nor, indeed, were the counties of Antrim and Down part of the Plantation of Ulster. The unexplained Flight of the Earls in 1607 resulted in the presumption of their disloyalty and in the confiscation of 'their' lands[1] which lay to the west of Ulster in what are today Counties Armagh, Londonderry, Donegal, Cavan, Monaghan, Tyrone and Fermanagh. These lands were apportioned to English, Scottish and even some Welsh undertakers but, in the event, the settlement proved to be largely Scottish.

The settlement took place gradually throughout the seventeenth century. Starting from small beginnings, it swelled to a torrent which eventually, in the following century, over-spilled into North America. This second wave of migrants – from Ulster to the New World – took with them many of the ideas produced by their sojourn in Ireland and these ideas are embedded in the Declaration of Independence.

What was different about the earlier migration to Ulster was that the migrants came in established groups, mainly from south-west Scotland, and gradually – it has been estimated that there were only about 4,000 Scottish families in Ulster by 1630 – they formed a cohesive community marked by certain distinctive religious and economic characteristics. Firstly, lowland Scotland at the Reformation had become Calvinist or Presbyterian and, secondly, the Scots were arable farmers whereas the Irish inhabitants tended to be pastoral farmers. In an important article in *Ethnologia Europaea* Dr Alan Gailey has estimated that there were probably some 33,000 Scots in the north of Ireland in 1659; and in 1685 it was estimated that of the minority Protestant population five-to-one were Scots. Assuming that the Presbyterian Church is the mark of the Scottish settlers, some idea of the spread of the Scottish settlements can be deduced from the place and date of the erection of Presbyterian congregations. The establishment of a congregation would indicate that the settlers had acquired a certain density and self-confidence. Before 1631 there were thirteen congregations, mainly in Down and Antrim, but by 1660 there were seventy and by 1688 one hundred and four, mainly spread through the Ulster lowlands. The 1690s were a period of severe famine in south-west Scotland; this produced another wave of migration and between 1691 and 1715 a further forty-four Presbyterian congregations were erected. Thus, one hundred and forty-eight congregations were established between 1613 and 1720 and a further six were added by 1740, giving a total of one hundred and fifty-four by the mid-eighteenth century.[2] In the seventeenth century most of the ministers of these congregations were Scots, but towards the end of the century there was a change and between 1691 and 1720 one hundred and twenty-nine future ministers were born in Ulster, usually in the well established Presbyterian areas.

An Irish Presbyterian congregation is not necessarily the equivalent of a parish but is rather a local group of like-minded people. They elect their minister who is chairman of the kirk session, an elected committee charged with advising and assisting the minister in the widely interpreted spiritual oversight of the congregation.[3] All the ministers in a given area meet in presbytery to which each kirk session also sends an elder. Throughout the eighteenth century all the northern presbyteries met as a whole in the Synod of Ulster and the southern presbyteries in the Synod of Munster. Synods and the General Assembly are enlarged presbyteries and are subject to the same concepts of democracy and consensus. They are presided over by an annually elected moderator. The Moderator of the General Assembly nowadays sits in a chair with *primus inter pares* (first among his equals) inscribed above it. He can speak for the Assembly only if it expressly gives him permission to do so; similarly, a minister cannot speak for his congregation unless so requested. At the same time, the opinion of an influential minister carries great weight. In the eighteenth century both Synods were guided by the General Assembly of the Church of Scotland. The General Assembly of the Presbyterian Church in Ireland, formed by the union of various groups of Irish Presbyterians, first sat in 1840. Because of the emphasis which it places on the individual's conscience, Presbyterianism has always carried with it the potential to fracture and it did so on a number of occasions in the eighteenth century. Then, as now, Presbyterians covered a wide spectrum of views and opinions. For example, when on one occasion Francis Hutcheson preached in his father's congregation at Armagh the result was uproar and the exit of the congregation. Hutcheson allegedly preached about:

> a gude and benevolent God and that the souls of the heathens themselves will gang to heaven, if they follow the licht of their ane consciences. Not a word . . . aboot the gude, auld, comfortable doctrines of election, reprobation, original sin and faith.[4]

In 1756 John Wesley, on one of his itinerant missions, wrote that:

> I spoke very plain at Lisburn, both to the great vulgar and the small. But between Seceders, old self-conceited Presbyterians, New Light men . . . it is a miracle of miracles if any here bring forth fruit to perfection.[5]

Schism or agreement to disagree is sometimes the price of independence.

Many, probably most, eighteenth-century Anglicans would actually have preferred Catholics to Presbyterians. Both Catholics and

Anglicans viewed society as a predetermined hierarchy, while Presbyterians structured it as a democratically elected oligarchy. Catholics were feared for their numerical strength, their potentially despotic Jacobite politics and their claims to estates now in Protestant hands. The Earl of Cork and Orrery probably expressed the views of the Protestant establishment when, writing in the middle of the century, he explained that:

> I held both presbyterians and Roman Catholics in the utmost abhorrence . . . I esteemed presbyterians . . . as cunning, designing, canting, ignorant hypocrites, and for Roman Catholics, I thought every one of them held a knife at my throat.[6]

Presbyterians were objectionable in themselves. Their unbending dislike of social or ecclesiastical hierarchy, their belief in consensus and even their perverted stoicism which discouraged the self-indulgence of effective public relations – an omission which has arguably plagued them to this day – were characteristics which set them apart.[7]

The Presbyterians and the government

Protestant unity barely survived the crisis of 1689-1692 precipitated by the Revolution. If the Catholic was a third-class citizen, the Presbyterian was a second-class citizen, caught between his dislike of Rome and his disapproval of Anglicanism. It was only in the nineteenth century that the word 'Protestant' came to refer to non-Catholics. Throughout the eighteenth century the word 'Protestant' referred to those who conformed to the established Church of Ireland. Presbyterians and other Protestant non-conformists were known as 'Dissenters'. The Protestant Ascendancy held to the view expressed by Sir Richard Cox in the 1690s. Cox was quite happy that people should go to heaven by the route of their choice but wished 'for the security of the Established Church to exclude from office, or any share in the government, all those who would not conform to the Church established by law'.[8] He did not achieve this during the reign of the Calvinist William III.

The union of the English and Scottish Crowns in 1603 had not resulted in the political union of the kingdoms, or in the creation of a common legal or a common ecclesiastical system, although England had periodically attempted to impose episcopal church government upon Scotland. Following the death of Queen Anne's last child in 1700, the burning question in English politics was the securing of a peaceful and united succession. In 1703 the Scots, having secured their system of church government in 1688, further fuelled the religious controversy then waging in England by, in their turn, refusing to tolerate Scottish Episcopalians and by insisting that the sincerely Anglican Queen of Scotland confirm their position by consenting to an Act for Securing the True Protestant and Presbyterian Government and an Act anent Peace and War. This latter statute highlighted the connection between the religious question and the succession. England and Scotland were at war with France and her allies for most of Queen Anne's reign and the Act stated that the Queen's successors could not declare war on behalf of Scotland without the consent of the Scottish parliament. They further underlined this separatism in an Act of Security declaring that, on the death of the Queen, the Scottish parliament would meet to select its own sovereign and indicating that, unless certain conditions were met, it was their clear intention to separate the two kingdoms still joined only by the accident of their common descent to a sickly woman who might well die before the conclusion of the war. The Queen delayed her consent to this Act until 1704 when she reluctantly gave way.[9] Three years later the treaty between England and Scotland which formed the Act of Union confirmed the separate Scottish ecclesiastical and legal systems and made Great Britain an economic unity. In return, the Scots agreed to a legislative union and a common succession. The Anglican establishment bitterly resented the terms of this agreement but they had to accept it.

The indemnity granted to Scottish Jacobites some months earlier, in the spring of 1703, presented a further complication for, on the Jacobites' return home, Scotland became a hotbed of real and imaginary plots and counter-plots. In November 1703 a friend of Ormonde, the Irish Lord Lieutenant, made a tour of the north of Ireland. He made a report to the Lord Lieutenant who ordered the Chief Secretary, Southwell, to forward it to the Earl of Nottingham. This document contained such lurid statements as: 'Mr Sterling (a Presbyterian minister) said that they "ought to cut the throat and kill every Englishman that came into this country"' and he concluded by inquiring whether 'just cause may be found to break' the Presbyterians. A few weeks later, on 18 January 1704, the Irish Penal Law was before the English Privy Council which added the test clause:

provided always, no person shall take benefit of this Act as a
Protestant . . . that shall not conform to the Church of Ireland as by
law established, and subscribe the Declaration and also take and
subscribe the Oath of Abjuration.

The addition of this clause undoubtedly bewildered many contemporaries. Many arguments, political and diplomatic as well as religious, were advanced to explain it. On 22 February the bill, An Act to
Prevent the Further Growth of Popery, came before the Irish parliament where, shortly before, the *regium donum* (a small grant paid to
the Presbyterians from the time of Charles II) had been abolished as
an unnecessary expense. After a debate of about two hours, centred
on the Test clause, the bill passed with not more than twenty negative
votes. The Catholics, represented by Sir Toby Butler and Sir Stephen
Rice, were heard *pro forma*. Butler recalled the services of the
Dissenters at Londonderry and Enniskillen, and remarked that 'if
this is all the return they are like to get, it will be but a slender encour-
agement, if ever occasion should require, for others to pursue their
example'.[10] However, the Presbyterian historian, James Seaton Reid,
viewed the situation rather differently when he wrote that:

it was a singular occurrence, an instance, perhaps, of righteous
requital, that they themselves after having given their aid in
Parliament to carry one of the most cruel of these statutes against
the Romanists should, by a clause added to that very statute, be
deprived of their own civil rights and subjected in their turn to serious grievances on account of their religion.[11]

Whether the Test clause originated from political circumstances,
ingratitude or divine retribution, it was as immediately and deeply
resented by the Presbyterians as the rest of the Act was by the
Catholics.[12] It widened and deepened the already existing fissures in
Irish society.

Although the government declared that 'the Queen was determined that Dissenters should not be persecuted or molested in the
exercise of their religion', the political stresses and the religious ani-
mosities of Queen Anne's reign were such that, at the time of the
Queen's death in 1714, the Presbyterian churches at Antrim,
Downpatrick and Rathfriland were closed and their doors nailed
up.[13] This was the only period of direct interference with the regular
practice of worship, but the prerogative courts of the established

Church continued to harass both clergy and laity over questions of marriage and inheritance until 1844. As late as 1842 an Irish Chief Justice stated that 'the law of this country does not recognize the Orders of the Presbyterian Church, because it is not episcopal'.[14]

This *de iure* denial of the ordination of Presbyterian clergy by the established Church continued throughout the eighteenth century. According to eighteenth-century legal opinion neither Catholic priests nor Presbyterian ministers existed in Ireland. However, as Catholic priests were episcopally ordained, the legality of Catholic marriages was never questioned by either the established Church or the State, but from time to time the established Church queried the legality of Presbyterian marriages and the consequent legitimacy of their offspring.[15] The Church of Ireland controlled the granting of probate and under certain circumstances marriages conducted under the discipline of the Presbyterian Church in Ireland remained illegal until after the notorious case of *Regina* v. *Millis* in 1844, which led to the situation being clarified in the Marriage Act.[16] Naturally the Presbyterian Church enjoined upon its adherents the desirability of marrying in accordance with its rites although, in addition to questions of inheritance, this could allow the unscrupulous to commit bigamy.

After the accession of George I life became easier for the Presbyterians although they did not acquire all the benefits which they had anticipated. The Sacramental Test was not repealed but the *regium donum* was restored and increased to £2,000 *per annum*. In 1719 a Toleration Act exempted Dissenters from the penalties of not attending services in the established Church and allowed their ministers to perform their pastoral duties without the liability of a £100 fine. At the same time a retrospective Indemnity Act was passed to protect Presbyterians who had offered military support to the government during the 1715 Rebellion when there had been fears of a Jacobite invasion of Ireland. This Act set the pattern for twenty-four similar Acts during the next fifty years, which alleviated to some extent the restrictions placed upon Presbyterians during the penal era.

After the accession of the Hanoverians the British government was quite willing to repeal the Test clauses but the Irish Church and parliament were adamant that they should stand. Archbishop King, writing in 1719, explained to the Archbishop of Canterbury that:

the true point between them and the gentlemen is whether the Presbyterians and lay elders in every parish shall have the greatest

influence over the people, to lead them as they please, or the land-
lords over their tenants. This may help your Grace in some degree
to see the reason why the Parliament is so unanimous against tak-
ing off the test.[17]

The government was always afraid that the Presbyterian ecclesiastical
structure would create a state within a state.

The end of the 1720s saw a period of famine and a wave of emigration to America. It has been estimated that at least 300,000 Ulster
Presbyterians emigrated to North America between 1718 and 1775.[18]
Among the reasons that the emigrants gave for going was the depriva-
tion of their civil and religious rights. Undoubtedly their motives were
complex: for instance, in 1735 a Tyrone migrant wrote home to his
minister that 'here aw [all] a man works for is his ane [own]';[19] and,
often after great hardship, these migrants were amazingly successful.
Whatever their motives, the government was worried by this decline in
the Protestant population, and between 1731 and 1733 Walpole, the
British Prime Minister, under Presbyterian pressure, tried to extend to
Ireland the lenient Whig policy towards Dissenters. He failed, and the
Test clause remained operative until 1780, probably for the reasons
given by Archbishop King in 1719. Even then it was altered only with
reluctance. As late as 1778, when the first substantial measure of
Catholic relief was granted, a clause rescinding the Test was struck out
by the British Privy Council which was anxious to separate the conces-
sions given to Catholics and Dissenters. Moreover, Presbyterian sympathy with the Americans, combined with their enthusiasm for
Volunteering, did not endear them to Lord North's administration.

Presbyterian education

Presbyterians have always placed great emphasis on education for
both religious and social reasons. John Knox's dictum of a school
beside each church is well-known and his new university of
Edinburgh, founded in 1560, was the youngest of the *four* ancient
Scottish universities, all established before James VI became King of
England. Only members of the Church of Ireland as by law estab-
lished could attend the University of Dublin. Education for the mini-
stry was therefore a problem for both Presbyterians and Catholics.
The latter were educated in the various Catholic colleges throughout
Europe but mainly in France, while the former were educated in
Scotland, the majority at the University of Glasgow. In order to par-

ticipate in a democratically elected form of church government Presbyterians required a high standard of education from both the laity and the clergy. They had at least to be able to read the Bible and were expected to be able to form an opinion upon the various theological arguments of the day.

The problems which confronted Protestant Dissenters in obtaining higher education, although similar to those confronting Catholics, were less acute and their solution was simpler. Nevertheless, the seriousness of the issue of higher education and its consequences has not been fully understood. Numerically the most powerful of the protestant non-conformist denominations, the Presbyterians were exposed to the greatest weight of official displeasure. In 1705 the Irish House of Commons passed a resolution stating:

> that the creating and continuing any seminary for the instruction and education of youth in principles contrary to the established Church and government tends to create and perpetuate misunderstandings among Protestants.[20]

In 1711, when the House of Lords petitioned the Queen to withdraw the *regium donum* from Presbyterian ministers, one of the reasons they gave was that the Presbyterians were using it 'to form seminaries to the poisoning of the principles of our youth'.[21] In fact the *regium donum* had never been used for this purpose and the Synod of Ulster counter-petitioned the Queen, declaring that it was:

> a great grievance to us that education of our youth is extremely discouraged by our being deprived in many places of the liberty of entertaining common schoolmasters of our own persuasion – not to mention seminaries, the want whereof obligeth us to send our youth abroad, to the public prejudice of the kingdom.[22]

Both the resolution of parliament and the petition of Synod were correct in their assessment of the issue and its consequences but, in failing to resolve it satisfactorily, they created a far more enduring problem and one with dangerous, imperial ramifications.

The majority of the Presbyterian clergy and the university-educated laity were *alumni* of the University of Glasgow. The remainder went to the three other Scottish universities, with Edinburgh next in popularity, while a few went to St Andrews and Aberdeen. Among the graduates of the Edinburgh Medical School were the United

An eighteenth-century view of the University of Glasgow which was attended by many Ulster Presbyterian students during that century; from an original drawing by an Ulster student, Andrew Craig (1754-1833), later Presbyterian minister of Lisburn.

Irishmen, Dr Thomas Addis Emmet and Dr William Drennan, while another Edinburgh graduate was Dr James MacDonnell, the founder of the Belfast Hospital. In 1764 Thomas Reid, then Professor of Moral Philosophy at the University of Glasgow, wrote to a friend that:

> Near a third of our students are Irish. Thirty came over lately in one vessel. We have a good many English, and some foreigners; many of the Irish as well as Scotch are poor, and come up late to save money.[23]

The Irish students often travelled over in groups which snowballed in numbers as they moved across Ulster until they arrived at Donaghadee in County Down. Here they took ship for the dozen or so miles across the narrow North Channel to Portpatrick and then walked about eighty miles to Glasgow.[24] When the Rev. Henry Cooke attended Glasgow University at the beginning of the nineteenth century, he found that:

> the Irish students were well known along the route especially on the Scotch side of the channel. Every house was open to them . . . Not infrequently their bed was an old arm-chair in the kitchen or a piece of carpet in the inner room.[25]

When Maynooth was established in 1795 the Synod of Ulster, supported by James Stewart, MP for County Tyrone, appointed commissioners to confer with the government with a view to establishing a university at Cookstown, County Tyrone; but this project came to nothing and the Presbyterians continued to go to the Scottish universities rather than to Dublin University, which was expensive by Scottish standards and, with its Anglican traditions and outlook, less acceptable.

'Calvinism', it has been said, 'is the creed of rebels'. The position, power and independence of the Church of Scotland, secured as part of the Act of Union of 1707, freed it from sporadic persecution. The heady mixture of democratic consensus and schism inherent in Presbyterianism combined with the intellectual climate of the scientific revolution and the Age of Reason to produce the Scottish Enlightenment. It was in this atmosphere that Ulster students at their most impressionable age came into their own and discovered that, however oppressed at home, in Scotland they were an accepted part of a vigorous intellectual establishment. Furthermore, in Francis

Hutcheson, Professor of Moral Philosophy at the University of
Glasgow from 1729 until his death in 1746, Ulster gave to the Scottish
Enlightenment one of its most charismatic and influential teachers.
Incidentally, Hutcheson was the first professor of Glasgow University
to lecture in English rather than in Latin.[26]

A licentiate of the Presbyterian Church in Ireland, Hutcheson was
the son and grandson of Presbyterian ministers. He was educated first
at Saintfield where his grandfather was minister, and then at James
McAlpine's famous academy at Killyleagh. In 1710, at the age of six-
teen, he entered Glasgow University where he was a pupil of the celebrated Professor John Simson. While Hutcheson was an
undergraduate, Simson, who was influenced by the Rev. Samuel
Clarke's semi-Arian views, incurred the wrath of the Scottish
Assembly by whom he was tried between 1714 and 1716 for teaching
Arian and Pelagian doctrines. In 1717 Hutcheson returned home
and was about to accept a call to become minister of Magherally congregation when he was invited to become principal of an academy in
Dublin. There he remained until he returned to Glasgow in 1729. In
accepting the position in Dublin he was undertaking some risk, par-
ticularly in view of Archbishop King's well known hostility to
Presbyterians, let alone the illegality of Presbyterian teachers.
However, while in Dublin Hutcheson (who was naturally diplomatic)
and King became friends. Both were members of the intellectual
circle which gathered round Robert, 1st Viscount Molesworth, at
Swords.[27]

Hutcheson became a considerable force in Glasgow University politics. For example, among other policies, he persuaded the University
of Glasgow to give students from some of the Irish academies
advanced standing and to allow them to take their arts degree after
two years' study at the university. Unfortunately the training given at
these academies varied and consequently the arts degree was open to
criticism.[28] Following the death of the Professor of Divinity in 1743,
Hutcheson had worked hard to secure the election of the liberal Dr
Leechman. Writing to the Rev. Dr Thomas Drennan, William
Drennan's father, he remarked that: 'We cannot be certain of the
event, but have good hopes. If he succeeds it will put a new face upon
Theology in Scotland'.[29] He succeeded. Leechman was elected by the
casting vote of the Rector and for the few years between Leechman's
election and Hutcheson's death in 1746 they made a formidable pair.

The Scottish Church represented many shades of theological opinion. The Presbytery of Glasgow watched over the faith and morals of

those employed in the university with vigilance. Hutcheson, like his own teacher Simson, had been called before them, accused of teaching two serious heresies: firstly, that it was possible to have a knowledge of good and evil without a knowledge of God; and, secondly, that the standard of moral goodness was the promotion of the happiness of others. He succeeded in satisfying the Presbytery but declared that he 'would as soon speak to the Roman conclave as to our Presbytery'.[30] Hence Leechman's appointment was of the utmost importance in the endless tug-of-war between the two sides of Presbyterianism.[31]

Two of Hutchesons students, Alexander Carlyle and Adam Smith, have left tributes to Hutcheson's charismatic skill as a teacher. Carlyle recollected that when he was a student in the 1740s:

the fame of Mr Hutcheson had filled the college with students of philosophy and Leechman's high character brought all the students of Divinity from the Western Provinces as Hutcheson attracted the Irish.[32]

In 1787 the University of Glasgow elected as its Rector its most distinguished son, the political economist, Adam Smith. On this occasion Smith wrote to the principal expressing his gratitude to the university which had taught him and afterwards had sent him to Oxford, writing of his subsequent academic career that:

soon after my return to Scotland, they [the Glasgow professors] elected me one of their own members; and afterwards preferred me to another office [Professor of Moral Philosophy], to which the abilities and virtues of the never to be forgotten Dr Hutcheson had given a superior degree of illustration.[33]

The influence of Hutcheson's teaching spread far. It should be viewed not only in purely philosophical terms but also in the light both of the nexus of Ulster-American migration and of the depth of the resentment felt, in the Ulster of Hutcheson's childhood, towards the government's treatment of the Presbyterians in the Ireland of Queen Anne. There is a dichotomy in the Presbyterian's outlook for, while religion is an individual matter, bad or unsatisfactory government is not a matter of bad or inefficient people but of a defective system which allows them to operate in an undesirable or tyrannical way. Hutcheson's teaching came to fruition in his contribution to the

Francis Hutcheson (1684-1746), the Ulster-born Professor of Moral Philosophy at the University of Glasgow (1730-1746) and the 'Father of the Enlightenment'. Hutcheson's teachings were highly influential not only in Scotland but also in Ulster and America. After a medallion by Antonio Selvi, courtesy of the Scottish National Portrait Gallery.

philosophy behind the American Revolution, for his students
included men like the Rev. Francis Alison, who came from the
Laggan in County Donegal. Benjamin Franklin appointed Alison as
Professor of Moral Philosophy in the College he founded at
Philadelphia.[34] Notes taken from Alison's lectures show how closely
his teaching followed that of Hutcheson, and no less than fifteen out
of the forty-six men who served in the Continental Congress from
1776 to 1783 were Alison's students. Hutcheson's theories included
the following propositions:

1. '. . . that civil power can scarce be constituted justly any other
way than by consent of the people: and that rulers have no other
sacred rights or majesty, than what may arise from this . . .'

2. 'If the mother-country attempts anything oppressive toward a
colony and the colony be able to subsist as a sovereign state by itself,
or have its plan of polity miserably changed to the worse: the colony
is not bound to remain subject any longer . . .'

3. '. . . the common interest of the whole people is the end of all
civil polity.'

4. '[that] . . . all power is vested in and consequently derived from
the people, that magistrates and rulers are their trustees and ser-
vants and at all times answerable to them.'[35]

Many of Hutcheson's students were appointed to important positions
not only in the Presbyterian Church in America but also in education,
in politics, in the law and, significantly, in publishing.

Presbyterians had long desired to establish a northern university[36]
which would replace Glasgow University in the education of their
youth. During the 1780s the Rev. Dr William Campbell, the minister
of Armagh, was involved in the abortive plan for an Ulster university
which was part of Chief Secretary Orde's scheme. In pleading his
cause, Campbell, with typical Ulster tact, suggested to Speaker Foster
that:

This would rouse the Genius of Trinity College and create a gener-
ous and manly competition which must produce the best effects
and carry on Dublin College to that excellence to which she is destined, for without Emulation there can be no excellence.[37]

The Duke of Portland thought that such stimulation was undesirable as, in his opinion, work was already overtaxing the health of the students of Trinity. More persuasively, Campbell pointed out that such a college could advance science and polite literature as well as applied mathematics, engineering and chemistry which would be 'of essential service to a country rising in trade and manufactures'.[38] But at the root of this movement lay a desire to establish institutions of sufficiently high standards to allow Presbyterian clergy to be educated in Ulster. When the university plan failed, the General Synod petitioned for a theological college, envisaged as state support for the development of Strabane Academy, then under the guidance of Dr Crawford.[39] Presbyterian radicalism undoubtedly discouraged government support and that, in turn, created a feeling of injustice which fuelled opposition, particularly in view of government's subsequent support for Maynooth.

NOTES

1. The land question in late sixteenth- and early seventeenth-century Ireland was complex; see, *A New History of Ireland. Vol. 3: Early Modern Ireland, 1534-1691* (Oxford: Clarendon Press, 1976) p. 187ff.
2. A. Gailey, 'The Scots Element in North Irish Popular Culture', *Ethnologia Europaea*, vol. 8, 1975; four maps, pp. 6-7, show the dissemination of Presbyterianism, 1611-1720.
3. J.M. Barkley, *The Eldership in Irish Presbyterianism* (Belfast: Barkley, 1963) esp. pp. 54ff. This short study gives some idea of the position of the Presbyterian Church in the community and the control it had over its adherents and also the support which it gave in a country with no Poor Law.
4. Quoted in J.S. Reid, *A History of the Presbyterian Church in Ireland*, new ed. (Belfast: Mullan, 1867) vol. 3, p. 294 n. 22.
5. N. Ratcliff (ed.), *The Journal of John Wesley* (London: Nelson, 1940) p.256; J.M. Barkley, *A Short History of the Presbyterian Church in Ireland* (Belfast: Presbyterian Church in Ireland, 1959) appendix 1, p. 118, gives a useful diagram of the various types of Presbyterian groupings, their unions and splintering.
6. Emily, Countess of Cork & Orrery (ed.), *Orrery Papers* (London: Duckworth, 1903) vol. 2, p. 254.
7. 'It has often been said of the Scotch-Irish that although they make history they leave to others the task of writing it, and this is largely true. The unfortunate part of it, however, is that the others who write history have often done so from a point of view unfriendly to this racial group': W.F. Dunaway, *The Scotch-Irish of Colonial Pennsylvania* (Chapel Hill: University of North Carolina, 1944) p. v.
8. Quoted in J.C. Beckett, 'The Government and the Church of Ireland under William III and Queen Anne', *Irish Historical Studies*, vol. 2, 1940-41, p. 282.
9. See C. Grant Robertson, *Select Statutes, Cases and Documents*, 9th ed. (London: Methuen, 1949) pp. 163-164; G.M. Trevelyan, *England under Queen Anne*

(London: Fontana, 1965) *Vol. 1: Blenheim,* p. 353, and *Vol. 2: Ramilles and the Union with Scotland,* pp. 246ff.

10. Quoted in Reid, *History,* vol. 2, p. 508.

11. Reid, *History,* vol. 2, p. 502.

12. The question of occasional (or nominal) conformity is a complicated one. Undoubtedly there were (at least nominal) conformers among both Catholics (documented in IMC Convert Rolls) and Presbyterians (e.g. MPs like William Cairns, MP for Belfast from 1703 to 1707), but although conforming lawyers did from time to time raise the ire of the Establishment the problem was limited, possibly *inter alia* by the extent to which communal pressure reinforced genuine belief. The success of the Penal Laws was a tribute to the sincerity with which both Catholic and Dissenters held to their convictions. There was nothing like the Occasional Conformity struggle in the England of Queen Anne, which culminated, after a number of failures, in a modified Occasional Conformity Act, 10 Anne cap. 6 (1711).

13. Reid, *History,* vol. 3, p. 56.

14. Chief Justice Pennefather, quoted in T. Croskery and T. Witherow, *Life of the Rev. A.P. Goudy, D.D.* (Dublin, 1887) p. 92.

15. Barkley, *Short History,* pp. 23-24, 55. Huguenots were similarly regarded by the Catholic Church in France; see, *French Historical Studies,* vol. 11, 1962, pp. 3-23.

16. Reid, *History,* vol. 3, pp. 486ff.

17. BL Add. MS 6117; C.S. King (ed.), *A Great Archbishop of Dublin, William King, D.D., 1650-1729...* (London: Longmans, 1906) p. 216.

18. Most eighteenth-century figures are guesses; this figure is given in I.M. Bishop, 'The education of Ulster students at Glasgow University during the eighteenth century', unpublished MA thesis, the Queen's University of Belfast, 1987, p. 111. The classic study is R.J. Dickson, *Ulster Emigration to Colonial America, 1718-1775* (London: Routledge & Kegan Paul, 1966); see also, *A New History of Ireland. Vol. 4: Eighteenth-Century Ireland, 1691-1800* (Oxford: Clarendon Press, 1986) pp. 32, 39-40.

19. Quoted in A. Lockhart, 'Some aspects of emigration from Ireland to the North American Colonies', unpublished M.Litt. thesis, University of Dublin, 1971, p. 45. The number of American Presidents of Ulster origins is one illustration of their success.

20. *Commons Jnl. Ire.* (Bradley ed.), vol. 3, p. 319, 1 June 1705; quoted in Reid, *History,* vol. 2, p. 519.

21. *Lords Jnl. Ire.,*vol. 2, pp. 410-411; quoted in Reid, *History,* vol. 3, p. 18.

22. Quoted in J.A. McIvor, *Popular Education in the Irish Presbyterian Church.* (Dublin: Scepter, 1969) pp. 31-32.

23. Quoted in H.G. Graham, *The Social Life of Scotland in the Eighteenth Century,* 2nd ed. (London: Blackie, 1901) p. 455 n. 3; Bishop calculates that between 1761 and 1780 the Irish students at Glasgow comprised 200 sons of tenant farmers, 77 sons of gentry, 3 sons of the nobility, 60 merchants' sons and 42 sons of the clergy, ibid. p. 125.

24. Bishop, 'Education', p. 141.

25. J.L. Porter, *Life & Times of Henry Cooke, D.D. LL.D.* (Belfast, 1875) pp. 15-16.

26. Reid, *History,* vol. 3, p. 296; J.M. Barkley, 'Francis Hutcheson (1694-1746)', *Bulletin of the Presbyterian Historical Society of Ireland,* no. 14, 1985; Bishop, 'Education', pp. 86ff.

44   E.M. JOHNSTON-LIIK

27. J.C. Beckett, *The Making of Modern Ireland, 1603-1923* (London: Faber, 1966)
    p. 184; McIvor, *Popular Education*, pp. 29-30.
28. Bishop, 'Education', p. 108; *Parliamentary Register*, vol. 1, Dublin, 1790, p.
    247, contains a reference to Scottish universities 'where degrees are to be
    obtained with so much facility, and with so little expense'.
29. Quoted in Bishop, 'Education', p. 104. Hutcheson, himself, had been
    elected by one vote in 1729 in a similar liberal v. conservative ballot.
30. Francis Hutcheson to Thomas Drennan, 16 April 1746, QUB Library
    Mic.B/39, no. 21, quoted in Bishop, 'Education', p.104.
31. Reid, *History*, vol. 3, pp. 294-300, discusses with balanced unfavourableness
    the views of both Hutcheson and Leechman.
32. Quoted in Bishop, 'Education', p. 103.
33. W.R. Scott, *Francis Hutcheson: his Life, Teaching and Position in the History of
    Philosophy* (Cambridge: Cambridge University Press, 1900). Hutcheson
    maintained a close interest in the Irish students, and there are detailed com-
    ments on a number of them in his correspondence. For instance, he
    remarked about one of them that: 'he is conceited, thinks himself a wit and
    scorns advice ... trifles away money and time for nothing'.
34. Dunaway, *Scotch-Irish*, pp. 223-224.
35. Bishop, 'Education', pp. 115-116.
36. ibid, pp. 144ff.
37. Campbell to Foster, quoted in Bishop, 'Education', p. 162.
38. Quoted in Bishop, 'Education', p. 163; for Portland's views see, W.E.H.
    Lecky, *History of Ireland in the Eighteenth Century* (London, 1892) vol. 5, p. 170,
    n. 2. Portland was hostile to the idea on principle.
39. Barkley, *Short History*, p. 42; A.T.Q. Stewart, *Belfast Royal Academy: the First
    Century, 1785-1885* (Belfast: Belfast Royal Academy, 1985) p. 20 reviews the
    suggestion that the Belfast Royal Academy should serve this purpose. Dr
    Robert Allen considered that this deprivation was a major cause of
    Presbyterian alienation at the end of the eighteenth century; see, Bishop,
    'Education', p. 174.

CALVINISM AND DARWINISM:
THE BELFAST-EDINBURGH AXIS

David N. Livingstone

On situating science and religion

In this paper[1] I want to address two things. Initially I should like to reflect briefly on some theoretical insights that arise from recent work in the history and sociology of science. I then want to deploy some of these ideas in an attempt to throw a little light on cultural connections between Ulster and Scotland. As a case study, I propose focusing on Victorian responses to Darwinism by Presbyterian intellectuals in Belfast and Edinburgh. Thereby I hope to disclose something of what I call the 'historical geography' of science and religion. In the present context, moreover, some scrutiny of these issues may serve to widen our consideration of cultural connection by attending to a dominating feature of modernity – though one frequently ignored by students of cultural life – namely, the scientific enterprise.

My project, moreover, is surely rendered all the more appropriate today by the fact that many of you will have passed by the statue at the entrance to the Botanical Gardens. It is, of course, that of William Thompson – Lord Kelvin – the Ulster physicist who spent a half-century at the University of Glasgow in a hugely impressive career that included a five-year presidency of the Royal Society. Men like Kelvin, and his brother James Thompson, together with figures like Thomas Andrews, James McCosh and Wyville Thompson, did as much, I suspect, in the production of an Ulster-Scottish scientific culture as did Francis Hutcheson and his Common Sense successors in the sphere of political life.

In recent years there has been a remarkable 'spatial turn' among students of society and culture. The genealogy of this twist of events is both multifaceted and complex. But among philosophers, social theorists and historians of science there has been a renewed emphasis on the significance of the local, the specific, the situated. Some philosophers thus argue that what passes as a good reason for accepting a particular belief differs from time to time and from place to place. What counts as rational, it turns out, is in large measure situation-specific. 'Good grounds' for holding a certain belief is evidently different for a twelfth century milkmaid, a Renaissance alchemist and a twentieth-century astrophysicist. Among social theorists there has also been a recovery of spatiality. The importance of the diverse locales within which social life is played out has assumed considerable significance with such writers as Clifford Geertz, Erving Goffman and Anthony Giddens. And, then again, there are figures like Michel Foucault and Edward Said who deploy spatial categories for rather different purposes. But survey is not my intention here. Rather it is to alert us to an increasing acknowledgement of the spatial in cultural life, an awareness that is being increasingly recognised among historians of science.[2] To put it another way, for all its claims to universality, science is also *local culture*. Thus, attention has been called to the role of experimental space – and its management – in the production of scientific knowledge, to the lines of diffusion along which scientific ideas and their associated instrumental gadgetry migrate, to the political geography and social topography of scientific subcultures, and to the institutionalisation and policing of the sites in which the reproduction of scientific cultures is effected. The cumulative effect of these investigations is to draw attention to the local, regional, and national features of science, an enterprise hitherto regarded as prototypically universal.

The implications of these recent developments for my present task are considerable. My suspicion is that the project of reconstructing the historical relations between science and religion might similarly benefit from a localising strategy that seeks to situate 'responses' or 'encounters' in their respective socio-spatial settings. To pursue such a programme, I suggest, will inevitably mean abandoning grand narratives that trade in abstract and idealist 'isms'. It will not do to speak of *the* encounter between, say, evangelicalism and evolutionism. Instead, I think we will be better advised to seek to uncover how *particular* religious communities, in *particular* space-time settings, developed *particular* tactics for coping with *particular* evolutionary theses. In this paper I want to make a preliminary stab at elucidating the responses of two sets of Calvinists to evolutionary claims in two different locales during the second half of the nineteenth century. If my argument is in the neighbourhood of a correct analysis, the specifics of these situations turn out to be of crucial importance.

Calvinists encounter evolution

During 1874, in two different cities, Presbyterian intellectuals with seriously similar theological commitments issued their judgments on the theories of evolution that were gaining ascendancy in the English-speaking scientific world. In Edinburgh and Belfast – both Calvinist heartlands – differing assessments of the new biology were to be heard; in these different situations varying rhetorical stances were adopted, for in these religious spaces different circumstances prevailed.

Two statements

Rainy in Edinburgh
In October of 1874 Robert Rainy, the new Principal of New College, Edinburgh – the theological college of the Free Church – delivered his inaugural address. His subject was 'Evolution and Theology' and, his biographer Simpson remarked, it 'attracted considerable attention'. According to Simpson:

> The religious mind of the day was disturbed about Darwinism and apprehensive lest it should affect the foundations of faith; and that a man of Dr. Rainy's known piety and orthodoxy should, from the Principal's chair of the New College, frankly accept the legitimacy of the application of evolution even to man's descent and find it a point on which the theologian 'may be perfectly at ease' reassured many minds.[3]

Indeed Rainy did make it clear that while some found evolution objectionable, he himself did not feel justified 'in imputing an irreligious position to the Evolutionist'. Accordingly, he insisted that even if 'the evolution of all animal life in the world shall be shown to be due to the gradual action of permanent forces and properties of matter' – a claim he himself actually doubted – that would have no bearing on 'the argument of the Theist [or on] the mind of a reverent spectator of nature'.[4] Indeed Rainy was even open to the possibility of an evolutionary account of the human physical form.

Porter in Belfast
That same winter in Belfast, J.L. Porter, Professor of Biblical Criticism in the General Assembly's College (and later President of Queen's

The Rev. Prof. Robert Rainy,
Principal of New College,
Edinburgh, who was
'perfectly at ease' with
evolution.

The Rev. J.L. Porter, Professor
of Biblical Criticism at the
Presbyterian College, Belfast,
who was disturbed by the
'crude theories' of the
Darwinians.

College), delivered the opening address to the Presbyterian faculty and students.[5] Here he ominously spoke of the 'evil tendencies of recent scientific theories' – and that of evolution in particular – which threatened to 'quench every virtuous thought'. The need for theological colleges was thus more urgent than ever so that 'heavenly light is preserved and cherished'. What was more, he declared that he was 'prepared to show that not a single scientific fact has ever been established' from which the pernicious dogmas of Huxley and Tyndall could be 'logically deduced'.[6] Within a few weeks, on the last day of November, Porter would pursue this same theme in an address on 'Science and Revelation: their Distinctive Provinces' which inaugurated a series of winter lectures on 'Science and Religion' in Rosemary Street Church in downtown Belfast. Here he inveighed against the 'crude theories and wild speculations' of the Darwinians. Empirically, he conceded, *The Origin of Species* had made 'one of the most important contributions to modern science'; in logic, by contrast, it was 'an utter failure'. In sum, the book was 'not scientific'. Darwin was not to be substituted for Paley.[7] In the key Calvinist spaces of Belfast and Edinburgh, different attitudes to evolution theory were already being promulgated.

Two situations

These key pronouncements, of course, were not elaborated in a vacuum. Rather they were broadcast in differing ideological contexts. My suggestion is that in these diverse arenas different issues were facing Presbyterian communities and that these issues were crucially significant in conditioning the rhetorical stances that were adopted by a variety of religious commentators on evolutionary theory. Besides this, different voices were being sounded in different ways and their modes of expression, whether bellicose or irenic, did much to set the tone of the local science-religion 'encounter'. I suggest that such prevailing circumstances – and no doubt there are many more – had an important influence on the style of language that was available to theologically conservative spokesmen pronouncing on evolution which in turn determined not only what could be *said,* but what could be *heard,* about evolution in these two different localities.

Edinburgh

In Edinburgh Robert Rainy attempted to 'retain the evangelical

heritage of the F[ree] C[hurch] while keeping pace with rapid contemporary developments', a strategy that increasingly made him a
controversial figure. To much of the secular press he became known
as 'Dr Misty as well as Dr Rainy', even though he was named by
Gladstone as the greatest living Scotsman. Later in his career, as an
ecclesiastical statesman and architect of the union of the Free Church
and the United Presbyterian Church, he found it necessary to 'offer
unlimited hospitality to biblical criticism'. And if in the case of
William Robertson Smith he judged it politic to sacrifice that
particular critic, he later protected Marcus Dods, A.B. Bruce and
George Adam Smith in a sequence of heresy trials, actions which
secured the later censure of those retaining the classical Calvinism
of the Free Church.[8] Certainly Rainy's *forte* was ecclesiastical
polity rather than intellectual engagement. But what *is* significant
is that, because, as Drummond and Bulloch put it, he 'was circumspect and heedful of public reactions', his endorsement of an evolutionary reading of human descent at New College in 1874 is
indicative of a general lack of anxiety about evolution among Scottish
Calvinists.[9]

In fact, during the 1870s in Edinburgh, the Darwinian issue paled
in significance beside two other intellectual currents assaulting the
orthodox Scottish mind. Of much greater moment than Darwinian
materialism[10] were biblical criticism and the influence of German
idealist philosophy.[11] As for the former, matters came to a head in
1876 when the protracted heresy trial of William Robertson Smith
began, litigation which would, in due course, result in his dismissal
from the Old Testament chair at the Free Church college in
Aberdeen. What had sparked off the matter was Smith's contribution
to the ninth edition of the *Encyclopaedia Britannica*, the 'canonical
expression', according to Alasdair MacIntyre, of the Enlightenment
thrust of contemporary Edinburgh high culture.[12] Smith's entry on
the 'Bible' revealed his espousal of the Graf-Wellhausen theory of the
Pentateuchal documents.[13] And this, together with the ninth edition's
progressivist ethos, threatened to subvert the traditional authority of
Scripture by promising to provide an architectonic overview of
knowledge.

In an environment where biblical criticism and idealist philosophy
were considered much more threatening than science – after all
Lord Kelvin was an Episcopalian of low church sympathies who regu-
larly worshipped in a Free Church congregation – these were the
arenas in which engagement was seen to be required.

Belfast

The situation was different in Belfast. On Wednesday 19 August 1874 the *Northern Whig* enthusiastically announced the coming of the 'Parliament of Science' – the British Association – to Belfast. Ironically, the meeting was being welcomed to the city as a temporary respite from 'spinning and weaving, and Orange riots, and ecclesiastical squabbles'. Nevertheless 'some hot discussions' were predicted 'in the biological section', between advocates of human evolution and those 'intellectual people – not to speak of religious people at all – who believe there is a gulf between man and gorilla'.[14] The Belfast meeting was to be what Moore and Desmond call 'an X Club jamboree' with its priestly coterie of Huxley, Hooker, Lubbock and, of course, Tyndall himself all speechifying.[15] If indeed an assault was to be mounted by the new scientific priesthood on the old clerical guardians of revelation and respectability, Scripture and social status, then what better venue could there be for a call-to-arms than the BA's meeting in Calvinist Belfast? Tyndall's pugnacious performance did not fall short of expectations. In an Ulster Hall garnished with accompanying orchestra he delivered – with nothing short of evangelical fervour – a missionary call to 'wrest from theology the entire domain of cosmological theory'. His conclusion was that all 'religious theories, schemes and systems which embrace notions of cosmogony . . . must . . . submit to the control of science, and relinquish all thought of controlling it'.[16] The gauntlet had been thrown down.

Events moved quickly. On Sunday 23 August Tyndall's address was the subject of a truculent attack by the Rev. Professor Robert Watts at Fisherwick Place Church in downtown Belfast. Watts, the Assembly's College Professor of Systematic Theology, had good reason for spitting blood. He had already submitted to the organisers of the Biology Section of the British Association meeting in Belfast a paper congenially entitled 'An Irenicum: or, a Plea for Peace and Co-operation between Science and Theology.'[17] They flatly rejected it.[18] It must have seemed to Watts that the scientific fraternity was not interested in peace. Yet the spurned lecture, which Watts – not prepared to waste good words already committed to paper – delivered at noon the following Monday in Elmwood Presbyterian Church, revealed just how enthusiastic he could be about science.[19] But the BA's rebuff *had* stung and chagrin over his expulsion from the programme put him in a bad mood. Yet this was nothing to the anger that Tyndall's address aroused in him. So when, on the Sunday following the infamous address, he turned his big guns on Tyndall in a sermon

Third Presbyterian Church, Rosemary Street, Belfast, the venue for much of the Presbyterian response to Tyndall.

preached to an overflowing evening congregation at Fisherwick Place Church in the centre of Belfast, the irenic tone of the rejected paper was gone. Tyndall's mention of Epicurus was especially galling; that name had 'become a synonym for sensualist', and Watts baulked at the moral implications of adopting Epicurean values. To him it was a system that had

> wrought the ruin of the communities and individuals who have acted out its principles in the past; and if the people of Belfast substitute it for the holy religion of the Son of God, and practise its degrading dogmas, the moral destiny of the metropolis of Ulster may easily be forecast.[20]

Watts, of course, was not a lone voice imprecating Tyndall-style science. On the very same Sunday that he was arraigning atomism before the downtown congregation of Fisherwick Place, the same message was buzzing through the ears of other congregations.[21] That evening none other than W. Robertson Smith found himself preaching from Killen's north Belfast pulpit. And, while he did not speak out there and then on Tyndall's speech, he had certainly caught the prevailing mood for he was moved within the week to write to the press challenging Tyndall's assertions about early religious history, castigating his 'pragmatic sketch of the history of atomism', and complaining that he was 'at least a century behind the present state of scholarship' concerning the Christian Middle Ages.[22] Small wonder that Tyndall reflected: 'Every pulpit in Belfast thundered of me'.[23] It was the BA event that set the agenda for Porter's opening speech at the Assembly's College that winter and for the Belfast response to evolution for a generation.

Two stories

Given the different sets of circumstances prevailing in Edinburgh and Belfast, it is now understandable why the subsequent histories of responses to evolution were different in these Calvinist cities. In a nutshell, the theory of evolution was absorbed in Edinburgh and repudiated in Belfast. Let me try to illustrate these diverging trajectories by reference to the judgments of a few key individuals.

Edinburgh: Adoption
Henry Calderwood was a key figure in Scotland's United Presbyterian

Church, retaining the modified Calvinism embodied in his Church's 'Declaratory Act' of 1879.[24] He was also a staunch defender of Scottish Common Sense philosophy and this enabled him to maintain philosophical continuity with the tradition of Scottish realism. This stance had involved him in a critique of the idealist inclinations of his teacher, William Hamilton. As Pringle-Pattison put it: 'Calderwood may be said to have been the first to reassert . . . the traditional doctrine of Scottish philosophy against the agnostic elements of Kantianism which Hamilton had woven into his theory'.[25] Calderwood's early work,[26] which appeared in 1854, established his philosophical reputation and, after serving as a United Presbyterian minister in Glasgow from 1861 until 1868, he was appointed to the Chair of Moral Philosophy in Edinburgh in 1868. Significantly, one of the first letters of congratulation was received from James McCosh – recently come to Princeton – who wrote enthusiastically of his appointment but also spoke of

> a dark thread running through the white of my feeling . . . I looked to you as my successor, and had laid plans to secure it. You would have had the support of the College and of my old pupils in the Presbyterian Church. As it is, I am now fairly at sea.[27]

Clearly McCosh had hoped that Calderwood would follow in his own footsteps and cross the Irish Sea to assume the Professorship of Logic and Metaphysics at the Queen's College of Belfast.

In the case of Calderwood (and indeed McCosh) the commonly held view that Common Sense philosophy was typically deployed against evolutionary theory certainly does not seem to hold good. In 1881, for example, he commended Darwin's work and insisted that the phrase the 'development of species' expressed an undoubted scientific conclusion, which had found a permanent place in biological science.[28] And that same year, in his Morse lectures delivered at Union Theological Seminary in New York on the subject 'The Relation of Science and Religion', he assured his hearers that Darwin's theory 'is no more at variance with religious thought, than with ordinary notions of preceding times' and that:

> the fewer the primordial forms to which the multiplicity of existing species can be traced, the greater is the marvel which science presents, and the more convincing becomes the intellectual necessity by which we travel back to a Supernatural intelligence as the source of all.[29]

And in the mid-1890s he asserted that 'Evolution stands before us as an impressive reality in the history of Nature',[30] for he was convinced that the evidence for 'descent with modifications' was

> so abundant and varied, as to leave no longer any uncertainty around the conclusion that a steady advance in organic form and function has been achieved in our world's history.[31]

Now, to be sure, none of this can be construed as unqualified endorsement for the Darwinian scheme. Throughout, Calderwood was insistent on the need for creative activity in the *origin* of life and for constant providential superintendence. *But* his rhetorical style was radically different from that of the Belfast Calvinists who, as we shall presently see, maintained an attitude of 'No Compromise!' with the new biology.

I have been dwelling for some time on the work of Henry Calderwood. But it would be remiss to ignore altogether the contributions of men like James Iverach, James Orr, Robert Flint, George Matheson and, of course, Henry Drummond. There is not space here, however, to recover the details of their pro-evolutionary sentiments. My purpose is simply to call attention to the widespread accommodationist strategies that were characteristic of Edinburgh's Presbyterian leadership.

Belfast: Repudiation

In Belfast, the Tyndall event cast terror into the hearts of solid Presbyterians for more than a generation. But there was still a sense that Tyndall's act of aggression was ultimately to be welcomed for it displayed to the world the machinations of the materialist school. It was precisely because he had spoken so plainly that the editor of *The Witness* (the weekly Presbyterian newspaper) could observe that: 'We now know exactly the state of matters, and what is to be expected from Professor Tyndall and his school, and we shall be able to take our measures accordingly.'[32] And measures the Presbyterian Church did take. Plans were hastily laid for a course of evening lectures to be given at Rosemary Street Church during the winter months on the relationship between science and Christianity. In time these addresses would be drawn together into a book, distributed on both sides of the Atlantic, under the title *Science and Revelation: A Series of Lectures in Reply to the Theories of Tyndall, Huxley, Darwin, Spencer Etc.*

During that 1874-1875 winter of discontent, the Presbyterian Church set out to stem, from Rosemary Street pulpit, any flood of materialism that Tyndall's rhetoric might unleash. Just as the villagers of medieval Europe and colonial New England annually beat the bounds – marked out the village boundaries – so the Presbyterian leadership needed to re-establish its theological borders. Indeed, it is precisely for this reason, I would contend, that the winter lecture series at Rosemary Street Church included ministerial addresses which made no specific reference to Tyndall, Darwin, Spencer, or any version of evolutionary theory. That they were included in the series attests to the perceived need to reaffirm systematically the cardinal doctrines of the faith so as to ensure that Presbyterian theological territory remained intact.

Just over a year earlier the Catholic serial, the *Irish Ecclesiastical Record,* had presented an evaluation of 'Darwinism' in which its correspondent castigated the 'Moloch of natural selection' for its 'ruthless extermination of . . . unsuccessful competitors', for its lack of evidence for transitional forms, for its failure to account for gaps in the fossil record, and for its distasteful moral implications.[33] As for the latest clash in Belfast, the Catholic archbishops and bishops of Ireland issued a pastoral letter in November 1874 in which they repudiated the 'blasphemy upon this Catholic nation' that had recently been uttered by the 'professors of Materialism . . . under the name of Science'. This certainly was no new warfare, they reflected; but the Catholic hierarchy perceived that this most recent incarnation of materialism unveiled more clearly than ever before 'the moral and social doctrines that lurked in the gloomy recesses of [science's] speculative theories'. Quite simply it meant that moral responsibility had been erased, that virtue and vice had become but 'expressions of the same mechanical force', and that sin and holiness likewise vanished chimera-like into oblivion. Everything in human life from 'sensual love' to religious sentiment were 'all equally results of the play between organism and environment through countless ages of the past'. Such was the brutalising materialism that now confronted the Irish people.[34]

The congruence between these evaluations and those of the Presbyterian commentators we have scrutinised is certainly marked. So why then should Watts, in a subsequent reprint of his pamphlet *Atomism: Dr. Tyndall's Atomic Theory of the Universe Examined and Refuted,* incorporate in an appendix 'strictures on the recent Manifesto of the Roman Catholic Hierarchy of Ireland in reference to the sphere of

Science'? That he wished to distance himself from their proposals is clear: it was 'painful', he noted, 'to observe the position taken by the Roman Catholic hierarchy of Ireland in their answer to Professors Tyndall and Huxley'.

The sectarian traditions in Irish religion doubtless had a key role to play in these particular machinations. The furore surrounding the Tyndall event merely became yet another occasion for Ulster nonconformity to uncover its sense of siege. In his confrontation with evolutionary theory Watts wanted to cultivate and tend to his own tradition's theological space, and not engage in extramural affiliations. And by seeking to cast secularisation and Catholicism as subversive allies against the inductive truths of science and the revealed truths of Scripture, he found it possible to conflate as a single object of opprobrium the old enemy – popery – and the new enemy – evolution. To Watts these were indeed the enemies of God – and of Ulster. Writing to an American friend, A.A. Hodge, in 1881 he observed:

> Communism is, at present rampant in Ireland. The landlords are greatly to blame for their tyranny, but the present movement of the Land League, headed by Parnell, is essentially communistic. He and his co-conspirators are now on trial, but with six Roman Catholics on the jury there is not much likelihood of a conviction.[35]

And later, in an 1890 letter to another American confidant, B.B. Warfield, on the eve of Gladstone's second Home Rule bill, in which he castigated both the Free Church and the United Presbyterians in Scotland, he added:

> Both these churches are so bent on Disestablishment that they are quite willing to sustain Mr. Gladstone's Irish policy & deliver their Protestant brethren into the hands of the Church of Rome, to be ruled by her through a band of unmitigated villains.[36]

For their part, the Catholic hierarchy did not miss the opportunity of firing its own broadsides at Protestantism. For the archbishops and bishops felt it would

> not be amiss, in connection with the Irish National system of education, to call attention to the fact that the Materialists of to-day are able to boast that the doctrines which have brought most odium upon their school have been openly taught by a high Protestant dignitary.

It only confirmed them in their uncompromising stance on the Catholic educational system. Had it not been for their own vigilance, an unbelieving tide would have swept through the entire curriculum. Such circumstances justified 'to the full the determination of Catholic Ireland not to allow her young men to frequent Universities and Colleges where Science is made the vehicle of Materialism'. Accordingly, the archbishops and bishops rebuked 'the indifference of those who may be tempted to grow slack in the struggle for a Catholic system of education'.[37] Tyndall's speech, it seems, succeeded not only in fostering the opposition of both Protestants and Catholics in Ireland to his own science, but in furthering their antagonism to each other.

As for Watts, he maintained his antagonistic attitude to evolution for the rest of his life. And by now, not surprisingly, he had grown entirely disillusioned with the Edinburgh New College network and enthusiastically cultivated links with Princeton. Writing to Warfield in 1889, he began:

> It would seem as if Princeton is going to absorb Belfast. Here I am asked to introduce to you, I think, the fifth student, within the past few weeks. Well, over this I do not grieve but rather rejoice. I am glad that our young men are setting their faces towards your venerable and orthodox institution instead of turning their backs upon orthodoxy and seeking counsel at the feet of men who are trampling the verities of Revelation under foot.[38]

In introducing yet another student to the Princeton campus he wrote to Warfield in 1893:

> I am greatly pleased to find that our young men have turned their eyes to Princeton instead of Edinburgh, and I owe you my warmest thanks for the great kindness you have shown them.[39]

Indeed he had already reminded Warfield that he had been writing a series of articles on the changing attitudes towards inspiration in the Free Church, reporting at the same time on the current hunting for heresy of A.B. Bruce and Marcus Dods. Predictably, Watts took a dim view of these teachers. 'How has the fine gold of the disruption become dim!' he sighed. 'The men of '43 would have made short work of these cases.'[40] And later that same year, having sent Warfield two days earlier a copy of his new book, *The New Apologetic; or, the Down-Grade in Criticism, Theology, and Science*,[41] he concluded yet another letter with the comment: 'I dread the influence of the Scotch Theological Halls, as you may learn from my book.'[42]

Watts's recollection of the Tyndall event remained unsullied and he neither would, nor could, release his grip on that bitter memory. Indeed, a full twenty years later he still recalled the details and, reflecting on it in a letter to Warfield, concluded:

> Dr. McCosh's successor in the Queen's College here, trots out Spencer to our young men in their undergraduate course, and one of my duties, in my class work, is to pump out of them Mill & Spencer.[43]

Managing theological space

In the latter decades of the nineteenth century, the intellectual leadership of the Presbyterian citadels of Edinburgh and Belfast were involved in the production and reproduction of theological space. In both, the field of discourse, which these figures had done so much to manage, set limits on the assertable: on what could be *said* about evolution and on what could be *heard*. In Edinburgh the concerns with biblical criticism, idealist philosophy, confessional modification in the wake of ecclesiastical reunions, and the pro-evolution sentiments of key leaders all made *rapprochement* with evolutionary theory intellectually congenial. In Belfast, the infamous BA meeting made it exceptionally difficult to be sympathetic to those who might argue that evolution could be construed in terms other than that of Tyndall's supposed philosophical naturalism. Besides, even if this possibility had been grasped, it would have been exceedingly difficult to *express* it in the doctrinal locality they had laboured so diligently to reproduce.

Local circumstances, I contend, are thus crucial to understanding how Ulster-Scottish Calvinists in these different places chose to negotiate their way around the issues that science seemed to be placing in one way or another on their agendas. To speak of an Ulster-Scottish cultural connection is, at once, to affirm both continuity *and* contestation. If, indeed, there is an Ulster-Scottish tradition, then we should perhaps recall that – as Alasdair MacIntyre insists – 'traditions when vital embody continuities of conflict'.[44]

NOTES

1. This paper is drawn from a longer, more detailed article in a forthcoming volume, *Evangelical Encounters with Science*, edited by Mark A. Noll, David N. Livingstone, and Darryl Hart (New York: Oxford University Press).
2. I have surveyed some of these matters in 'The spaces of knowledge: contributions towards a historical geography of science', *Society and Space*, vol. 13, 1995, pp. 5-34.
3. Patrick Carnegie Simpson, *The Life of Principal Rainy*, 2 vols, (London: Hodder and Stoughton, 1909) vol. 1, p. 285. A.C. Cheyne agrees, commenting that the pro-evolution sentiment of Rainy and Robert Flint 'is a measure of the rapid intellectual transformation that had taken place in Scotland in less than half a century': A.C. Cheyne, *The Transforming of the Kirk: Victorian Scotland's Religious Revolution* (Edinburgh: St Andrew Press, 1983) pp. 77-78.
4. Robert Rainy, *Evolution and Theology: Inaugural Address* (Edinburgh: Maclaren & Macniven, 1874) pp. 6, 9.
5. I have discussed the Belfast Calvinist response to Darwin in 'Darwinism and Calvinism: the Belfast-Princeton connection,' *Isis*, vol. 83, 1992, pp. 408-428; and 'Darwin in Belfast' in John W. Foster and Helena Ross (eds), *Nature in Ireland: A Scientific and Cultural History* (Dublin: Lilliput Press), forthcoming.
6. J.L. Porter, *Theological Colleges: Their Place and Influence in the Church and in the World; with Special Reference to the Evil Tendencies of Recent Scientific Theories. Being the Opening Lecture of Assembly's College, Belfast, Session 1874-75* (Belfast: Mullan, 1875) p. 8.
7. J.L. Porter, *Science and Revelation: Their Distinctive Provinces. With a Review of the Theories of Tyndall, Huxley, Darwin, and Herbert Spencer* (Belfast: Mullan, 1874) pp. 3-4, 5, 20, 22.
8. K.R. Ross, 'Rainy, Robert' in Nigel M. de S. Cameron (ed.), *Dictionary of Scottish Church History and Theology* (Edinburgh: T & T Clark, 1993). For such reasons he remained suspect – as did James Orr – to figures like John Macleod of the Free Church who interpreted Scottish theology to American Calvinists in his lectures at Westminster Theological Seminary. See, John Macleod, *Scottish Theology in Relation to Church History since the Reformation* (Edinburgh: Free Church of Scotland, 1943).
9. Andrew L. Drummond and James Bulloch, *The Church in Victorian Scotland, 1843-1874* (Edinburgh: St Andrew Press, 1975) p. 234.
10. Simpson maintains that Darwinian materialism did not 'greatly affect Scottish thought': Simpson, *Rainy*, vol. 1, p. 406.
11. See, Andrew L. Drummond and James Bulloch, *The Church in Late Victorian Scotland, 1874-1900* (Edinburgh: St Andrew Press, 1978) chap. 5, 'The Mind of the Church', pp. 215-297.
12. Alasdair MacIntyre, *Three Rival Versions of Moral Enquiry: Encyclopaedia, Genealogy, and Tradition* (London: Duckworth, 1990) p. 18.
13. See the discussions in Simpson, *Rainy*, pp. 306-403; Cheyne, *The Transforming of the Kirk*, pp. 44-52; and Richard Allen Riesen, *Criticism and Faith in Late Victorian Scotland: A.B. Davidson, William Robertson Smith and George Adam Smith* (Lantham: University Press of America, 1985) pp. 94-251.
14. *The Witness*, 19 August 1874.
15. Adrian Desmond and James Moore, *Darwin* (London: Michael Joseph, 1991) p. 611.
16. John Tyndall, *Address Delivered Before the British Association Assembled at Belfast, with Addition* (London: Longmans, Green, 1874). See the discussion in Ruth

Barton, 'John Tyndall, Pantheist: a rereading of the Belfast Address', *Osiris*, 2nd series, vol. 3 , 1987, pp. 111-134.

17. Robert Watts, 'An Irenicum: or, a plea for peace and co-operation between Science and Theology' reprinted in his *The Reign of Causality: a Vindication of the Scientific Principle of Telic Causal Efficiency* (Edinburgh: T. & T. Clark, 1888), pp. 1-26.
18. *The Witness*, 9 October 1874.
19. *Northern Whig*, 25 August 1874, p. 8; also, *The Witness*, 9 October 1874.
20. Robert Watts, 'Atomism: an examination of Professor Tyndall's Opening Address before the British Association, 1874' reprinted in his *The Reign of Causality*, pp. 27-43.
21. Rev. John MacNaughtan at Rosemary Street Presbyterian Church, Rev. George Shaw at Fitzroy, and Rev. T.Y. Killen at Duncairn, all took up the cudgels.
22. Robertson Smith, 'Letter', *Northern Whig*, 27 August 1874.
23. Cited in Barton, 'John Tyndall'.
24. Biographical details are drawn from W.L. Calderwood and David Woodside, *The Life of Henry Calderwood* (London: Hodder and Stoughton, 1900).
25. A. Seth Pringle-Pattison, 'The Philosophical Works' in Calderwood and Woodside, *Life of Henry Calderwood*, p. 423.
26. Henry Calderwood, *The Philosophy of the Infinite* (London: Macmillan, 1854). Calderwood was also the author of the popular student text, *Handbook of Moral Philosophy* (London: Macmillan, 1888). By 1902 it had gone through fourteen editions.
27. Cited in Calderwood and Woodside, *Life of Henry Calderwood*, p. 159.
28. Henry Calderwood, 'Evolution, physical and dialectic', *Contemporary Review*, vol. 40, December 1881, pp. 865-876, (pp. 867-868).
29. Henry Calderwood, *The Relations of Science and Religion* (New York: Wilbur B. Ketcham, 1881) pp. 21, 134-135.
30. Henry Calderwood, *Evolution and Man's Place in Nature* (London: Macmillan, 1893) p. 340.
31. Henry Calderwood, *Evolution and Man's Place in Nature*. 2nd ed. (London: Macmillan, 1896) p. 33.
32. 'The British Association', *The Witness*, 28 August 1874. It should not be assumed that there were no less strident voices. Rev. George Macloskie, in a letter to the *Northern Whig* on 26 August, for example, insisted that there was no desire in Belfast 'to stifle free scientific inquiry': *Northern Whig*, 27 August 1874, p. 8.
33. J.G.C., 'Darwinism', *Irish Ecclesiastical Record*, vol. 9, 1873, pp. 337-361.
34. 'Pastoral Address of the Archbishops and Bishops of Ireland', *Irish Ecclesiastical Record*, vol. 11, November 1874, pp. 49-70.
35. Letter, Robert Watts to A.A. Hodge, 1 January 1881, Archives, Speer Library, Princeton Theological Seminary.
36. Letter, Robert Watts to B.B. Warfield, 18 June 1890, Warfield Papers, Archives, Speer Library, Princeton Theological Seminary.
37. 'Pastoral Address'.
38. Letter, Robert Watts to B.B. Warfield, 23 September 1889, Warfield Papers, Archives, Speer Library, Princeton Theological Seminary.
39. Letter, Robert Watts to B.B. Warfield, 5 October 1893, Warfield Papers, Archives, Speer Library, Princeton Theological Seminary.
40. Letter, Robert Watts to B.B. Warfield, 18 June 1890, Warfield Papers, Archives, Speer Library, Princeton Theological Seminary.

41. In a postcard to Warfield dated 11 February 1891, he reported to Warfield that 'Spurgeon's "Sword and Trowel", "Expository Times", "United Pres. Mag." & "The Theological Monthly" have all given most flattering reviews of my "New Apologetic &c.".'

42. Letter, Robert Watts to B.B. Warfield, 13 October 1890, Warfield Papers, Archives, Speer Library, Princeton Theological Seminary. These same sentiments were also expressed in a letter of 31 May, the following year. Of course he dreaded no less the inroads biblical criticism was making in the United States too and chose to provide a detailed critique of Briggs's biblical theology in his opening address to the Assembly's College in November 1891. See, Letter, Robert Watts to B.B. Warfield, 22 July 1891, Warfield Papers, Archives, Speer Library, Princeton Theological Seminary.

43. Letter, Robert Watts to B.B. Warfield, 20 February 1894, Warfield Papers, Archives, Speer Library, Princeton Theological Seminary.

44. Alasdair MacIntyre, *After Virtue: a Study in Moral Theory*, 2nd ed. (London: Duckworth, 1985) p. 222.

HISTORY AND POLITICS

SCOTTISH RADICALISM AND THE 'BELFAST PRINCIPLE'

E.W. McFarland

Come here my frien's an' gie's your han',
Although we're from a neighbouring lan',
We for the cause of truth will stan',
And fight till we die in the morning.[1]

This piece, 'Friendship; or Wallace's Last Wish', was penned by an Ulster rhymer for a Scottish audience. With its death-or-glory rhetoric, it might be assumed that it dates from the Home Rule crises of the late nineteenth and early twentieth centuries, an era marked by the loyalist community's attempts to gain fraternal support from Scotland, an ancient nation to which they felt bound by kinship and common Protestantism.[2]

Its real context is very different. 'The cause of truth' in the poem is not the legislative Union, but Tom Paine's 'Rights of Man' and the 'frien's' are not the Union's defenders, but the 'Brother Friends of a Reform', radicals who were engaged in building a democratic movement in late eighteenth-century Scotland. To this group Ulstermen were drawn not just by cultural and religious familiarity but by a shared vision, an outward-looking and challenging blend of rationalist Presbyterianism and political liberalism which contemporaries knew as the 'Belfast Principle'.

This 'sentimental' relationship was given organisational expression in the alliance which developed in the 1790s between the Society of United Irishmen and Scottish reformers. The discussion which follows will look more closely at the intellectual and political roots of this alliance and will also examine the tensions which arose from attempts to build bridges between two societies which, while sharing many cultural affinities, displayed salient differences in terms of political and social development.[3]

This is a difficult task. With the exception of Marianne Elliott's path-breaking work, the international aspect of late eighteenth-century radical activity has generally remained underdeveloped in orthodox historical scholarship.[4] In the popular imagination too, both in Ulster and Scotland, awareness of this older political linkage between the two societies has faded. In the former case this is not unexpected for, as Walker has suggested, the Scottish connection has traditionally been fashioned and re-fashioned to suit the political exigencies of the day.[5] Meanwhile, in Scotland, the most enduring legacy of cross-fertilisation with Ulster has not been the rationalism and toleration of the radical alliance but the popular Protestantism of the Orange Institution, which also became rooted in Scotland in the 1790s.[6]

However, focusing on the radical alliance is useful to the historian. In the first place, it opens up important comparative issues and highlights the constraints facing democrats in Scotland. Both movements shared similar dynamics, feeding off a fluid international situation. Yet radicalism was always the more potent force in Ulster, owing to the province's greater economic dislocations and social fluidity, and to the tensions and uncertainty implicit in the Irish constitutional link with England. Indeed, it was the very optimism of the United Irishmen which attracted the Scots as they contrasted the difficulties facing large-scale democratic mobilisation in their own country.

Secondly, the 1790s are also an instructive period for studying the Ulster presence in Scottish political life. Irish migration has generally been viewed as synonymous with the economic migration and settlement of a Catholic population. This decade introduces an earlier, political dimension to population movement with the forced exile of both Catholics *and* Protestants across the North Channel. Some of these migrants continued to make a contribution to the politics of their country of origin, being intrinsic to the formation of a new radical tradition in Scotland in a period of rapid economic and social upheaval.[7]

An intellectual community

The United Irishmen were decided cosmopolitans. Not only did they seek to bind their own countrymen in a 'brotherhood of affection' but, inspired by the French Revolutionary ideals of fraternalism, their toasts and addresses exulted over every manifestation of democratic spirit from London to Warsaw.[8] Yet it was their counterparts in Scotland to whom Ulster radicals turned when seeking practical support for their reforming mission. This strategy drew on a pattern of long-standing reciprocal contact between the two Presbyterian societies, enabling the Belfast United Societies to greet the Scots in the spirit of 'the solemn ties of religion and blood [with] which many of us are connected with you'.[9] In other words, radicalism in this case was more than a mere reflection of events in France for, besides feeding on domestic grievances, it was able to draw on a historic core of beliefs in which the Scottish contribution was substantial.

By the late eighteenth century, a strong material basis had developed for sustained cultural and intellectual cross-fertilisation between Ulster and Scotland. Against the general background of demographic growth and economic expansion, the communications infrastructure improved and business relationships flourished.[10] A tangible product of increasing contact was migration. Again, this was a reciprocal process with Scottish mechanics engaged for Ulster firms, and Ulster weavers and bleachers imported into the Scottish linen industry.[11] This traffic moved increasingly in Scotland's favour as mechanisation in the north-eastern counties of Ulster threatened livelihoods. Soon the 'Scotch-Irish' were forming an identifiable community in Scotland's growing urban centres.

Besides these labour migrants, who were later to have their own role in promoting radical links in the 1790s, there was another key group. These were students, usually Presbyterians and mostly the sons of Ulster tenant farmers or Presbyterian ministers, who received their education at the universities of Glasgow and Edinburgh.[12] This group was to prove one of the most effective conduits for the transmission of radical social values into Ulster.

Ulster Presbyterians were excluded in practice from Trinity College, Dublin, through its Anglican tests for matriculation and graduation, but the Scottish colleges also had positive advantages in terms of accessibility and economy.[13] Parents were also attracted by the colleges' rising reputation for offering a progressive and practical education in tune with their denominational sensibilities. This in turn reflected the universities' responsiveness to the quickening intellectual climate in Scotland and beyond, with Enlightenment ideas beginning to flourish in the classrooms from the 1720s onwards.

A commanding presence here was Francis Hutcheson, Professor of Moral Philosophy at the University of Glasgow from 1729 to 1746.[14] Hutcheson's life, thirty years spent in Ireland and twenty-two in Scotland, was itself testament to the two societies' material and cultural intimacy. His political thought, too, refined earlier Covenanting Presbyterian ideas in line with the broader current of European rationalism.

William Drennan (1754-1820) founder and inspiration of the United Irishmen and author of the 'Irish Address' to his Scottish fellow-radicals; from a painting by Robert Home. Reproduced by courtesy of the Ulster Museum.

Hutcheson's main philosophical assumptions were the reasonable, social and altruistic nature of man, and the existence of a natural law to which the laws of the state must bend and by which all free men were informed through their 'moral sense'. From this stemmed two key convictions. The first was the inalienable right of freedom of opinion and religious tolerance. The second was an insistence on the right to resistance against tyranny. For Hutcheson the trust between ruler and ruled was broken if the potential 'utility' of civil society was not realised and if government no longer served the public good. In these circumstances, political rebellion might be preferable to continued subjection.

These were radical ideas which retained considerable longevity beyond Hutcheson's early death. They were transmitted from one generation of thinkers and educationalists to the next in a variety of contexts, from colonial America to Ulster, drawing their power not only from the clarity of Hutcheson's original exegesis but also from their applicability to real situations. In the case of Ulster Presbyterians, their receptiveness to Hutcheson's ideas stemmed chiefly from their sense of 'separateness' as a distinct community excluded from full social and political participation. It is, of course, impossible to quantify exactly the impact of the 'Scotch ideas', but there is ample, individual testimony as to the impact which distinguished teachers like Hutcheson could exercise on their students long into their adult life. William Drennan, the Belfast-born physician and poet, who has been assigned the key role in the foundation of the United Irishmen, maintained a long-standing friendship and correspondence with his former mentor at Edinburgh, Professor Dugald Stewart, which replicated his father's relationship with Francis Hutcheson in the previous generation.[15] Although Hutcheson had been dead over two decades, his influence clearly still weighed prominently in family and university circles, helping to mould the young man's politics. Drennan was duly proud of his radical Presbyterian heritage, proclaiming, 'I am the son of a Protestant dissenting minister, in the town of Belfast; the friend and associate of good, I may say, great men: of Bruce, of Duchal, and of Hutcheson'.[16]

We are obviously concerned here with an educated elite, but radical thought does seem to have enjoyed a generalised influence which extended beyond the university-educated. The widespread involvement of Presbyterian artisans and tenant farmers in political activity in the 1790s, particularly in Antrim and Down, may indicate, for example, that in many cases radical middle-class views were received sympathetically. Certainly, the pulpit, to which many products of the Scottish universities were called, was a powerful instrument for the propagation of ideas.[17]

There was, however, a final, negative aspect to the transplantation of Scottish intellectual currents to an Ulster context. Between the two main currents, Presbyterianism and Enlightenment, existed a vital tension. For running contrary to the expansive universalism of Enlightenment thought, was an older exclusiveness, rooted in Calvinism and exhibited with special relish in opposition to Roman Catholicism.[18] In the case of the Ulster Presbyterians, this exclusivism had the potential to become a dynamic force. This was partly through the alienation of the Presbyterian community from the structures of authority, which cast them easily in the role of a persecuted elite, 'a people among the nations', but also drew on a sensitive sectarian balance, particularly in the border counties. The presence of a significant Catholic population there gave 'anti-Popery' the practical focus it lacked in eighteenth-century Scotland. Indeed, liberal ideals of tolerance and fears of Catholic encroachment could easily coexist within Ulster Presbyterianism, both tendencies drawing on the Scottish intellectual legacy, a consideration only imperfectly and temporarily resolved by Irish radicals.

Building an alliance

Contact between the United Irishmen and the Scottish Friends of the People began within weeks of the Scottish group's establishment in July 1792. According to a government spy, who was already ominously monitoring the Irish organisation, this was signalled at a meeting on 31 August. A member present reported that he had private letters

> from some Scotch delegates lately assembled in Edinburgh who are determined to give up the idea of a partial reform of their burghs and join in demanding a *radical reform* of the whole *representation* of the *people* . . .[19]

At the United Irishmen's next meeting, a draft of a letter to the new 'Scotch Reform Society in Edinburgh' was read and referred to the Committee of Correspondence, with the final version ordered to be forwarded immediately at the meeting of 2 November.[20]

We do not know the individuals involved in initiating this connection. Yet, this is perhaps less important than the impression it conveys of the intensely personal character of radical activity. These were men who could confidently address each other from the vantage point of a broadly similar social status, upbringing and education. They had attended university together and had been members of the same student clubs. Just as the 'political nation' was small and byzantine in the late eighteenth century so was the world of those who aspired to join it.[21]

By this point, however, a subtle but significant shift had taken place in the relationship between radical thinkers in the two societies. The Scots were now destined to be junior partners in the radical alliance. Whereas it had been Ulster Presbyterians who had looked to Scotland for liberal education, now Scottish democrats looked to the 'Sister Isle' for a galvanising example of an enlightened reform movement.

The explanation for this is a simple one and rooted in the different political trajectories of Ireland and Scotland in the 1780s. It was the former which displayed greater strength and maturity of political protest activity. Here, both rural unrest and extra-parliamentary political activity by the urban middle class were gaining ground from mid-century, as the economic strains of Ireland's colonial status and the contradictions of Anglo-Irish constitutional relations became increasingly exposed. By the 1780s, traditional mechanisms of control were being tested and the authorities surveyed with anxiety the increasing alienation of literate public opinion from the parliamentary system.

The key organisation here was the Volunteers. Formed in Ulster in 1778, to supplement Ireland's ramshackle defence arrangements, within two years it had become a mass movement, campaigning for the restoration of legislative rights to the Irish parliament by means of a highly public campaign of reviews and assemblies. This pressure apparently achieved striking success as reform measures were rapidly put in motion. In Scotland, by contrast, the hegemony of the landed elite carried more decisive weight for their material advance and practical political power had been guaranteed by parliamentary union. Consequently, radicals had a narrower and more fragile base on which to build any political movement. The Scottish urban crowd could be ferocious when roused, but agrarian tensions and the tradition of middle-class political protest were each muted. The Scottish burgh and county reform movements were pallid indeed compared to the Volunteers whose apparent political triumph built the confidence of the 'Protestant nation' in the ability of peaceful mass protest to circumvent parliament.

The new political movements of the 1790s, despite sharing affinities in ideology and class composition, were also marked by these unique local circumstances. The origins of the United Irishmen lay in the impatience of Ulster Presbyterian radicals, schooled in the Volunteers' tradition, with the tameness and temporising of existing movements for reform. Amid a climate of drift during September 1791, the advanced reformers William Drennan and Wolfe Tone evolved plans for a committed reforming brotherhood which would harness progressive opinion and reconcile Protestant and Catholic. The United Irishmen's growing reputation as an intellectual and political powerhouse during the course of the next year removed the need to win over more moderate reformers. Timid spirits thus stayed adrift from the new movement which nevertheless proved adept at utilising existing channels of popular opinion for its own ends.

This auspicious beginning as a vanguard body, and its ability to use the organisational muscle of established reform movements, was not shared by the Scottish Friends of the People. Far from providing an alternative to caution and moderation, one of the main motivations of the leadership of the Scottish organisation was to control the tide of popular protest and to replace dangerous Painite doctrines with solid constitutional principles. From the outset, the aim was not to outflank existing movements like the Burgh Reformers but to unite them in a comprehensive national reform movement. This kept the new organisation firmly on the path of self-restraint.

Against this background, it is hardly surprising that some Scottish democrats found greater political inspiration in the United Irishmen. In the columns of Belfast's *Northern Star,* which circulated in Scotland, or their own *Edinburgh Gazetteer,* news of the progress of the United Irishmen became directly available. The latter's inaugural edition in November 1792, for example, featured a lengthy analysis of the Irish political situation in which Scottish readers were promised that the country, before a few months had elapsed, might boast 'a free, not mercenary army of 10,000 volunteer citizens'.[22] Yet, the very 'advanced' nature of public protest in Ireland could also be problematic, breeding a sense of superiority over those, like the Scots, who could not boast such enlightened positions as themselves.[23] Boundless confidence could also lead to the Irish offering stratagems, such as the linking of political radicalism with nascent nationalism, which were more suitable to their own situation than to that of the Scots.

This negative potential was realised within months of the forging of radical links. Solemn fraternal greetings, resolutions and correspondence played an important psychological role in bolstering a shared sense of grievance and purpose.[24] It was one of these productions from 'the immortal pen' of William Drennan which was to help upset the delicate internal balance of the Scottish reformers' organisation and bring down the wrath of the Scottish judiciary.

The address, 'To the Delegates Promoting a Reform in Scotland', was sent by the Dublin United Irishmen to be read at the first national convention in December 1792.[25] The difficulty with Drennan's 'Scotch letter' stemmed from its high-coloured 'nationalistic' tone which seriously alarmed moderate Foxite delegates who considered that it contained 'high treason against the union betwixt England and Scotland'.[26] Although the United Irishmen were still far from republican nationalists, the constitutional uncertainty of the 1780s had made them much less inhibited in questioning existing constitutional arrangements than the Scots whose romantic, literary patriotism was by no means equivalent to a desire to renegotiate national rights.

In fact, while the United Irishmen hoped that the uplifting sentiments of the address would 'flatter' the Scots out of their tactical timidity, the piece was as much for domestic consumption.[27] Tensions had developed within the Irish movement between a Dublin-based clique, led by Drennan and Hamilton Rowan, who viewed the Society as a high-profile, campaigning body, and those, like Wolfe Tone and Thomas Russell, who wished to broaden the democratic network beyond the urban elites.[28] The address was one of a number of productions by the former group as they tried to clarify their ideas and throw out a public challenge to government. Ulster radicals, however, seem to have been more aware that the Scots should not be unthinkingly incorporated into this provocative strategy. As the *Northern Star* had commented only a few weeks earlier:

> the Scots seem not to be behind hand in the pursuit of Freedom; but we would be sorry to find that they would thus prematurely push into violent measures without making application to the legislature for redress.[29]

Essentially the difficulty for the address was that, while Ireland was reaching a peak of optimism by December 1792, in Scotland the situation for radicals was an increasingly delicate one. The Friends of the People were undecided on their movement's direction. For some enthusiasts in the Scottish reform movement, such as Thomas Muir, the main promoter of the 'Irish Address' in Scotland, the role of the

Thomas Muir, Edinburgh advocate, Scottish radical, and self-proclaimed United Irishman sentenced in August 1793 to fourteen years' transportation. Reproduced by courtesy of the National Galleries of Scotland.

first Friends of the People Convention was originally to inspire and concentrate the reform process after the model of the Irish Volunteers' assemblies.[30] For Whiggish moderates, the Convention was intended to produce a coordinated national policy. In the event, both interpretations were overtaken by external developments. The radicalisation of the revolution in France towards the end of the year, coupled with continuing popular unrest at home, encouraged the authorities to harness the nervous energy of Scotland's propertied classes by means of a flood of loyal addresses and a subsidised press.[31] Thus the most pressing task of the Convention became to refute loyalist charges of treachery by a display of restraint.

When the 'Irish Address' was introduced to the Convention by Muir it duly unleashed two days of bitter dispute. Against minority demands, it was agreed to return the 'elegant piece of declaration' to its author for 'smoothing'.[32] Yet the refusal of a public reading did nothing to stem the loyalist backlash and the effects of Drennan's address continued to reverberate for the Scottish democrats.

Indeed, the offensive intensified with the outbreak of war with Revolutionary France in February 1793. 'Universal brotherhood' had become identified with sympathy for an enemy power, and the first major target was Thomas Muir. His championing of the 'Irish Address' had already provided the authorities with the perfect judicial weapon and he was tried for sedition in August 1793. Still glorying in Drennan's words and defending the United Irishmen from the dock, he personally provided the collateral evidence for his conviction. 'The Sidney of his Age', as the *Northern Star* lauded him, was sentenced to fourteen years' transportation, informing the court that he was himself now a member of the United Irish Society and that, in the last moments of his life, to have been so would be 'my honour and my pride'.[33]

Muir's trial marked a watershed for radicals. Their 'just and common cause', originally the product of easy optimism and fraternal ideals, was now a strategic imperative. As a matter of urgency, more formal organisational links began to be forged, not only with the United Irishmen but also with English radical societies. The instrument of this new cooperation was the British Convention, an assembly of delegates from the three kingdoms, projected for October 1793 to demand the full democratic agenda of universal suffrage and annual parliaments. The new defiance in its proceedings was signalled in the reading of a new address, this time from the four Societies of United Irishmen in Belfast. Its sentiments were more forthright and pugna-

cious than the original paper. At the very outset, the Belfast men's
internationalist vision was expounded, as they beheld:

> The vivid glow of patriotism which brightens the face of other
> nations, and the irresistible elasticity, with which man, long bent
> down into a beast of burden, shakes off the yoke of despotism and
> resumes his form erect in neighbouring kingdoms. We exult in the
> triumph of humanity which regenerated Gaul exhibits . . . We
> accompany with raptures, the steps of freemen traversing the
> mountains of Savoy, erecting the standard of liberty on the strong-
> holds of despotism . . .[34]

Perhaps not all of the address was as welcome to Scottish ears. The
past intellectual glories of Scotland, 'where a Reid and a Beatty broke
the spells of an annihilating philosophy', were contrasted to 'her present degenerated state, as a nation sleeping over her political
insignificance . . .' and, with a characteristic touch of Ulster Presbyterian hubris, the audience was reminded that, however humili-
ating their own situation in that province, 'the Protestants and the
reformed among us, in the sense of freedom, were much superior to
the Scottish people'.[35] Although the address received no formal reply,
the very fact that this spirited piece could now be read without the
drama surrounding its predecessor illustrates the path by which
radical solidarity was coming to be accepted as a political necessity
by the Scots. This was given formal expression in the establishment
of a committee to draw up a plan of general union between the
Scottish and English movements, but the United Irishmen were also
drawn in, as a touchstone of fraternal bridge-building, the
Convention resolving that their members be admitted to speak and
vote in their assembly.[36]

The contrast with the vacillation of the previous year was now complete. The United Irishmen, particularly their most radical elements,
were delighted and, well aware of the seachange which had occurred,
moved quickly to consolidate this new closeness by making delegates
of the British Convention and its constituent assemblies full members
of their own society.[37]

Such was the tempo of events in the early 1790s, however, that their
high spirits were quashed almost immediately by a renewed government offensive. Its effects were felt most severely in Scotland where
the Convention was forcibly dispersed on 6 December 1793. This
reverse caused disagreement in United Irish ranks but, just as the

leaders of their Dublin organisation began to criticise the Scots for their pusillanimity, the official campaign turned against their own movement. Other members, notably two Ulster visitors, were more phlegmatic, and sympathised with the Scots' plight. Dr James Reynolds of Tyrone defended them, saying that they 'only waited for the proper time', as indeed did his own people of the north. Meanwhile Samuel Neilson, the *Northern Star*'s editor from Belfast, was insistent that correspondence be maintained. Not wishing to transact business through the Post Office, in the light of possible measures against 'treasonable correspondence', he suggested that he had 'some very *confidential friends* in Edinburgh, happy in forwarding any United Irish papers to any part of Scotland'.[38]

Missionising and migration

Government had predictably failed to recognise the Scottish and Irish reformers' hunger for openness and orderly protest. As Neilson's plans for the secret passage of material between Ulster and Scotland suggested, the future of the radical alliance now lay in the hands of a developing revolutionary underground whose tactics gained a practical boost from interwoven domestic and international crises, signalled by the escalation of official coercion and France's shift on to the military offensive from the end of 1794.

The United Irishmen were still the dominant force in the alliance. By the early summer of 1795 they were evolving into a militant republican movement, again making use of existing radical societies but also determined to extend their new conspiratorial system and insurrectionary strategy throughout Ireland and on to the British mainland. Here, Scottish radicalism seemed apparently well-adapted in organisational terms to become an effective political underground. For all its limitations, the Scottish Friends of the People Association had entailed a centrally coordinated, nationwide network which compared favourably with the more dispersed English pattern of metropolitan and provincial societies. Culturally too, the Presbyterian legacy of independent thought suggested a closer approximation with conditions in Ulster.

Yet these initial advantages were offset by structural weaknesses, for the United Scotsmen, as the new covert organisation was to become, were to find chronic difficulty in capitalising on economic discontent sufficiently to secure a mass membership. Unlike the United Irishmen, the Scots were destined to remain something of a revolutionary elite in their own country, with perhaps only a few thousand members even at their height.[39]

By the summer of 1795, the Belfast United committees were again considering extending their operations to Scotland. Neilson, Henry Joy McCracken and William Putnam McCabe, the cadre of leaders who have been identified as leading the radicalisation of the United Societies that year, were anxious to send an agent to Scotland:

> . . . thinking the People ripe for revolt and this a fit citizen for their use, and in consequence of a *Plan* provided by the B. Com[ee] [Belfast Committee] he was to traverse Scotland as a *Highland Piper*. He learned the tongue and was to have gone from town to town to organise a General Insurrection, from there to the South of Ireland (Cork), hence to *Paris* to enlist the French.[40]

Although they drew back at the last moment from this rather fanciful enterprise, it is indicative of the breadth of the Belfast men's ambitions.[41] Two more serious phases of missionising were to follow during the next two years, each fuelled by episodes of government repression. Thus in 1796 the spy, Bird, was soon reporting that Samuel Neilson and Samuel Kennedy, chief compositor of the *Northern Star* and founder of the Irish Jacobin Club, 'were connected with Jacobin Clubs in Kinsale, England and Scotland'.[42] 'Men of confidence' had already been sent over in July 'with new Irish constitutions for the inspection and approbation of the Scots'.[43] Significantly, efforts here followed the organisation of the borderlands of Ulster and developed simultaneously with preliminary missionising work in Connacht and Munster. The thinking of the Belfast men may have reflected cultural as much as geographical proximity, with Scottish radicals providing a more comfortable reference point than some of their fellow countrymen.

Despite subsequent reports that 'the Scotch were not possessed of sufficient energy', missionising continued strongly into 1797.[44] Indeed, in the turmoil of that year Ulster radicals had little choice. A narrowly averted French landing at Bantry Bay at the end of the previous year led to a new government offensive which concentrated on the province, sapping United Irish organisation there by arrests and forcible disarming. Despite their hopes of further French intervention in the near future, the Dublin leadership counselled delaying any domestic military effort until French assistance had assumed a concrete form. The Ulster committees now began to display a growing capacity for independent action. Missionising offered an outlet for their restless energy which the drift of policy from the south denied them. Not only did external contact raise their morale during a period of enforced inactivity but it was also considered useful in negotiations for French support, if the the prospect of a diversionary landing on the mainland could be held out.

Although it was English population centres which proved to be the magnet for the most prominent agents, the Ulster United men had various advantages in their more discreet efforts to externalise their movement across the North Channel. The established educational channels which existed between the two societies lay open for exploitation, an obvious cover for United Irish ideas being the flow of Ulster Presbyterian students into the Scottish universities: one Tyrone student, James Boyle, arrived in Glasgow with 'a purse, collected from the local United men, for the purpose of making United Scotchmen'.[45] Economic links between Ulster and the west of Scotland were also at a premium. A tradition of seasonal labour for harvest time was well established in the western counties by the end of the eighteenth century. Elsewhere in Scotland, peripatetic hawkers of Irish linens and cheap cloth were a familiar sight, as were a swelling complement of Irish beggars and vagrants.[46] This itinerant population could provide a useful cover for United work, much as they did throughout Ireland where pedlars and packmen were also employed directly to disseminate radical literature.

Besides these transients, the United Irishmen were also able to benefit from a developing process of permanent migration and settlement in Scotland. In Wigtownshire, Kirkcudbright and Dumfries there had been 'some mixture from time immemorial', and large numbers of Irish had begun to settle in Ayr and surrounding parishes from the 1770s, with Girvan and Maybole becoming major receiving centres for migrants towards the century's end. In Glasgow, the population was sufficient by 1792 to sustain a Hibernian Benefit Society.[47] The west was not alone in this respect, and Ulster linen weavers also contributed to a sudden rise in the population of Fife around the same time, with Perth and Forfar also affected.[48] The resultant migrant communities could be pressed into service as operational bases for underground activity. In south Ayrshire, for example, the Lord Lieutenant reported that those gathered as weavers in villages in the locality formed 'a serious body of disaffected, who would take the first opportunity upon alarm of trying everything in their power to bring on mischief'.[49]

Voluntary labour migration was only one dimension of population movement from Ulster. The government strategy of disarming and of targeted coercion greatly boosted the tide of migrants, some motivated by the generally unsettled state of the province, others by the need to flee from direct persecution.[50] The tide of arrivals rose in line with the intensification of military action, often amounting in one day from '100 to 150 men in a Body' who then were liable to melt away in every direction through the western counties.[51] This influx was vital for the fortunes of the United system in Scotland. It meant that the conscious policy of the Belfast leaders to select and finance agents was no longer the only means of propagating their beliefs and tactics, but was now complemented by the spontaneous testimonies of those who had experienced at first hand the military campaign in Ulster.

The subversive potential of this population movement was well understood by the Scottish authorities and, although they faced less of a domestic challenge than their Irish neighbours, fears of 'contagion' were to heavily influence their calculations. These were indeed well-founded. By March of 1797, government intelligence was becoming slowly aware of a shadowy new radical grouping, the United Scotsmen, where United Irish influence was highly significant.

The United Irish contribution was seen most clearly in the new Scottish group's hierarchical, oath-bound structure. As the Lord Advocate was well aware, this marked a conscious reshaping of Scottish radicalism in the Irish image.[52] Yet this was not a simple Irish 'takeover'. Missionising from the Ulster societies was not the sum total of external influences on the Scots, for links with England had also survived from the days of the British Convention.[53] It would also seem that radical politics in Scotland possessed a greater internal momentum than elsewhere on the British mainland. The United Scotsmen drew on the same occupational groups which had formed the grassroots of the Friends of the People.[54] What the United system offered these local groups, however, was a systematic new method of organising radical activity and disseminating ideas and, above all, the sense of belonging to a wider radical community.

For the Scots, this international dimension was vital, given their failure to attract significant numbers at home. This fact had been brought home during the riots against the Militia Act in the summer of 1797. These had boosted United Scottish activity in rural areas and had demonstrated growing tensions between ruler and ruled. Yet power relationships retained sufficient flexibility to ride out the crisis. The Scottish authorities were able to pursue an effective strategy in which determined military action was combined with attempts to organise support for the raising of a militia. This in turn curbed the United Scotsmen's ability to integrate popular grievances into sustained support for their own political agenda.[55] Again, Ireland offers an instructive contrast. Here anti-militia riots in 1793 resulted in five times the casualties incurred in the agrarian disturbances of the previous thirty years. This episode signified the final bankruptcy of the 'moral economy', creating an atmosphere of fear and repression which the United Irishmen were able to draw on when building their mass movement.[56]

If these domestic constraints were not enough, fundamental difficulties also arose with the arrangements for attracting French support. Scottish radicals now realised that, when military aid was was the prize, the United Irishmen's role as mediators between Scotland and France became plagued with contradiction as international brotherhood was rapidly pushed aside in the struggle over scarce resources. The position of United emissaries in Paris, like Wolfe Tone, was indeed an awkward one following Ireland's failure to rise after the Bantry Bay expedition at the end of 1796. When French interest did revive it became apparent that any Irish venture was to be subsumed in a general British invasion attempt. For Tone this meant that the potential for disaffection in England and Scotland was being given greater weight than the real organisation they had painfully constructed in Ireland. They had also to accept that the whole missionising campaign of the Ulster committees might actually have damaged their own cause by directing French resources elsewhere. Not surprisingly, Tone was highly sceptical, for example, of the imaginative scheme of the Dutch general, Daendels, in 1797 to make a direct attempt on Scotland, and was delighted when two Ulster agents offered a 'very rational' appraisal of the results of their efforts in Scotland:

> It seems that emissaries have been sent from the north of Ireland to that country, to propagate the system of United Irishmen; and that they have to a certain degree, succeeded in some of the principal manufacturing towns, such as Paisley and Glasgow, where societies are already organised, and by last accounts they have even advanced so far as to have formed a provincial committee: nevertheless they observed these facts rested on the veracity of agents sent from the north, the Scotch having sent none of their body in return; that they could not pretend to say whether the Scotch patriots were up to such a decided part, as to take up arms in case of

an invasion, but their opinion rather was they were not so far advanced.[57]

Conclusion: 'A just and common cause'

The Ulstermen's brutally honest assessment sat uneasily with the morale-boosting pronouncements usually made for domestic consumption.[58] In Scotland too, a new realism had come to characterise radical activity generally as radical cells in old democratic centres, such as Perth and Paisley, struggled on in the face of increasingly well-informed government counter-measures. By June of 1798 their determination seemed rewarded as the long-awaited United Irishmen's rebellion had at last broken out.

In fact, the course of the 1798 rebellion was to be as destructive for Scottish radical hopes as any of the authorities' efforts. The '98 was a ferocious, uncontrolled episode. Lacking in appropriate leadership, debilitating internal splits opened up over the direction of the proposed rising and it broke out spontaneously. It swiftly degenerated into chaotic sectarian slaughter, amply demonstrating the persistence of deep social fissures between Catholic and Protestant which the United Irishmen had desperately wished to bridge. Despite rumours on the Portpatrick packet that, 'the people of Scotland were as hostile to government as those in Ireland, and were up in great numbers', Scottish participation in the '98 was not as 'brother-friends' but as members of the Crown forces under orders to defeat the United Irishmen in the field.[59] Scottish troops, and Highland Fencible regiments in particular, formed a disproportionate number of the 30,000-strong regular force stationed in Ireland on the eve of the Rebellion, totalling thirteen out of twenty regiments.[60] This was a possibility foreseen by one Belfast United Irishman who had explained that there were only three things that they were dreading: 'a bad harvest, the exportation of victuals, and the importation of Scotch soldiers'.[61]

While there is evidence that a few Scottish democrats were encouraged by the United Irishmen's spectacular blow against government, more commonly the defeat in Ireland appears to have damaged the United Scotsmen's self-belief, as the bloodshed of the Irish rebellion brought home to them what 'revolution' could mean in practice.[62] The failure of the French to provide substantial aid was disappointing but even more sobering was the savagery of the conflict and the spectre of sectarian murder, almost inconceivable after the messages of universal brotherhood delivered by their United allies over the past seven years. Nor could they easily turn to those allies for support. The 1798 Rebellion was a massive defeat for the United Irishmen. Although the movement and Irish popular disaffection outlived the attempt, the unique moment which had joined domestic pressures to the demands of French military strategy had passed and with it the United Irishmen's best opportunity. Official links were now overshadowed by the contribution of 'freelance' agents and, amid the ever swelling flow of migration from the northern counties, contact between the two groups of radicals became more haphazard.

Increasingly in the new century, radicals in Scotland were to be forced back on to their own resources. By no means, however, was this the end of the United legacy. Having already exercised a formative influence in the shaping of democratic politics in Scotland, the inspiration of Irish radicalism persisted in terms of outlook, organisation and personnel.

In the first place, the internationalist impulse was far from quenched. The expansive concept of brotherhood which had so discomfited the Friends of the People Convention in 1792 was now a commonplace in radical rhetoric.[63] Solidarity also had a more tangible expression. When a combination of operative weavers was formed in Glasgow and its vicinity in 1809, almost instinctively the new association corresponded with different associations in England and Ireland.[64] The latter initiative was understandable as Ulster was suffering from similar fluctuations in cotton manufacture, with half of the factories in the Belfast area idle by 1814.[65] Personal ties may also have been instrumental: the operative weavers in the west of Scotland included, in the Lord Advocate's view, 'a considerable body of Irishmen, disposed to riot and tumult', but they were fortunately kept quiet and peaceable by their native Scots colleagues.[66] Local Irish support was certainly evident towards the end of 1812 when 40,000 weavers eventually went on strike after a series of legal wrangles over wage rates.[67]

Open tactics were not the only option. As the government remained implacably set against reform and as economic distress intensified in the aftermath of the Napoleonic Wars, the alternative for some radicals was to follow the underground insurrectionary path. For this an organisational blueprint, in the old United Irish system, and a body of experienced personnel lay ready to hand in the industrial communities of the west of Scotland. By 1816 secret committees were meeting in the west, drawing in both 1812 activists and even survivors from the 1793 Societies.[68] 'The constitution of

Masonry and Masonic signs' were employed as security devices, but the need was apparently felt for a more disciplined approach. 'Copies of the arrangements of the Irish insurgents and of the traitors in Scotland in 1795' were compared, with the Irish model being the one selected. Partly, this promised 'a regular and disciplined force' to allow arming to begin but again some of the Glasgow leaders may also have been personally acquainted with the United Irish system.[69] Some of those involved in the new organisation were Ulster migrants: the committee met in the house of the weaver Hugh Dickson, who had left County Tyrone in 1800; and his colleague Andrew McKinlay, another weaver, was a native of County Armagh, who had come to Scotland in 1799.[70] McKinlay, indeed, appears as a driving force behind the secret initiative, producing a copy of the United Test and declaring it would serve as an oath of fidelity.[71] Yet events had moved on since 1798 and the searing experience of the sectarian polarisation of the United Irishmen's rebellion had clearly left its mark. On this occasion the old oath was not to be an inclusive 'Bond of Union', for McKinlay decreed that Roman Catholics were not to be allowed into the association:

> because priests had preached against all interference in political matters and auricular confession made the associates afraid that Roman Catholics might be the means of betraying them.[72]

Transplanted to Scotland as a by-product of migration, these confessional complexities were to colour the Irish presence in Scotland for the next century and beyond. They remained, however, lost on the authorities. For grandees like Lord Advocate Hope and the Duke of Hamilton, the growing Irish population, regardless of their actual religious and political allegiances, was the enemy within, 'almost all of the most suspicious character, and very many of them known to be old rebels, not in the least reformed'.[73] Likewise, for many ordinary Scots who had been able to follow its course in the loyalist press, the '98 had been 'a real popish rebellion'. Irishmen were 'croppies', rebels by definition, and immediately suspect and threatening to the public peace.[74] In this way, relations between the Scots and Irish were destined to fall far short of the death of 'puerile antipathies between races' which had inspired the original architects of the radical alliance.

NOTES

1. 'Friendship; or Wallace's Last Wish' in R.R. Madden (ed.), *Literary Remains of the United Irishmen of 1798 and Selections from Other Popular Lyrics of their*

Times... (Dublin: Duffy, 1887) quoted in L. Lunney, 'Ulster attitudes to Scottishness: the eighteenth century and after', in Ian S. Wood (ed.), *Scotland and Ulster* (Edinburgh: Mercat Press, 1994) p. 60.

2. G. Walker, *Intimate Strangers: Political and Cultural Interaction between Scotland and Ulster in Modern Times* (Edinburgh: John Donald, 1995) pp. 17-55.

3. These themes are explored fully in E.W. McFarland, *Ireland and Scotland in the Age of Revolution: Planting the Green Bough* (Edinburgh: Edinburgh University Press, 1994).

4. For Elliott's work see, 'The "Despard Conspiracy" reconsidered', *Past and Present*, no. 75, 1970, pp. 46-61; 'The origins and transformation of early Irish republicanism', *International Review of Social History*, vol. 23, 1977, pp. 405-428; *Partners in Revolution: the United Commission* (New Haven; London: Yale University Press, 1982); and *Wolfe Tone: Prophet of Irish Independence* (New Haven; London: Yale University Press, 1989). For a contrary approach, see, R.B. McDowell, *Ireland in the Age of Imperialism and Revolution, 1760-1801* (Oxford: Clarendon Press, 1979).

5. Evident, for example, in the use of Covenanting imagery during the Home Rule period; see Walker, *Intimate Strangers*, p. 13.

6. E.W. McFarland, ' "A Mere Irish Faction": Orangeism in nineteenth-century Scotland', in Wood (ed.), *Scotland and Ulster*, pp. 71-72.

7. For a challenging view on this contribution from the 1830s, see, J. McCaffrey, 'Irish issues in the nineteenth and twentieth century: radicalism in a Scottish context' in T. M. Devine (ed.), *Irish Immigrants and Scottish Society in the Nineteenth and Twentieth Centuries* (Edinburgh: John Donald, 1991) pp. 116-137.

8. See H. Joy and W. Bruce (eds), *Belfast Politics; or, a Collection of the Debates, Resolutions and Other Proceedings of that Town in the Years 1792 and 1793* (Belfast, [1794]).

9. JC 26/280, Scottish Records Office (SRO); also reprinted in Joy and Bruce (eds), *Belfast Politics*, pp. 100-104.

10. L. Cochran, *Scottish Trade with Ireland in the Eighteenth Century* (Edinburgh: John Donald, 1985).

11. R.R. Madden, *The United Irishmen: their Lives and Times*, series 2 (London, 1857-1860) vol. 2, p. 43; Walker, 'The Protestant Irish in Scotland' in Devine (ed.), *Irish Immigrants*, pp. 45-46.

12. I.M. Bishop, 'The education of Ulster students at Glasgow University during the eighteenth century', unpublished MA thesis, the Queen's University of Belfast, 1987.

13. For Edinburgh University see: D.B. Horn, *A Short History of the University of Edinburgh, 1556-1967* (Edinburgh: Edinburgh University Press, 1967) p. 120. William Drennan was aware that he could have got his medical degree at Glasgow on 'so much easier terms' but that an Edinburgh degree was more 'credible': M. McTier to W. Drennan, 25 January 1778, no. 21; and W. Drennan to M. McTier, 7 February [1778], no. 22; Drennan Letters, T. 765, Public Record Office of Northern Ireland (PRONI).

14. For further biographical details see: W. Leechman, 'Some account of the life, writings and character of the author' prefixed to Hutcheson's posthumous, *A System of Moral Philosophy* (Glasgow, 1775); W. R. Scott, *Francis Hutcheson: his Life, Teaching and Position in the History of Philosophy* (Cambridge: Cambridge University Press, 1900).

15. Letters from Dugald Stewart and Mrs H. Stewart to W. Drennan, 1807-1808, DE. 1. 1002, H5-8, University of Edinburgh Library Special Collections; see also Drennan Letters, T. 765, PRONI, for frequent mentions of his friend.

16. W. Drennan, *Fugitive Pieces in Verse and Prose* (Belfast; London, [1815]) pp. 192-193.

17. The right to private judgement, a cornerstone of Protestantism, further permitted dissension from the minister's sermonising. This was dramatically demonstrated when one of William Stavely's congregation protested so violently at what he considered a seditious sermon that he later died of apoplexy: Samuel Ferguson, *Brief Biographical Sketches of some Irish Covenanting Ministers* ... (Londonderry: Montgomery, 1897) p. 33.

18. C. Camic, *Experience and Enlightenment: Socialisation for Cultural Change in Eighteenth-Century Scotland* (Edinburgh: Edinburgh University Press, 1983) pp. 15-18.

19. Rebellion Papers 620/19/97, National Archives of Ireland (NAI).

20. Contact was also initiated with the London Friends of the People: Rebellion Papers 620/19/97; 620/19/100; 620/19/104, NAI.

21. Thomas Muir, Secretary of the Edinburgh Friends of the People societies, for example, attended Edinburgh University from 1785 to 1787, and there joined the progressively-inclined Speculative Society where his membership overlapped with Thomas Emmet, a prominent member the Dublin United Society. William Drennan had been a member of the same society during his studies at Edinburgh in 1778. James Mackintosh was well aware that this phenomenon had its ironies. Three of his old friends in the Edinburgh Speculative Society were Baron Constant de Rebeque, Charles Hope and Thomas Addis Emmet. Their subsequent fortunes were 'a curious specimen of the revolutionary times' in which he had lived. 'When I was in Scotland in 1801, Constant was a tribune in France; Charles Hope was Lord Advocate; and Emmet, his former companion, a prisoner under his control': R.J. Mackintosh, *Memoirs of the Life of Sir James Mackintosh* (London: Moxon, [1835]) vol. 1, p. 27.

22. S. Nenadic, 'Political Reform and the "ordering" of middle-class protest' in T.M. Devine (ed.), *Conflict and Stability in Scottish Society, 1700-1850* (Edinburgh: John Donald, 1990) pp. 65-82.

23. As William Drennan wrote of the Scottish political scene in the 1780s: 'They have made some attempts at Volunteers in this country, but they are rude and imperfect structures... time will show. I wish these defensive Caledonian bands every possible success': W. Drennan to M. McTier, September 1782, no. 44, Drennan Letters, T. 765, PRONI.

24. As the young William Cobbett commented: '*The press was suffocated with their addresses,* and letters of fraternity, which were swallowed by *the mob,* for whom they were intended, with an appetite which generally characterises that class of citizens': Cobbett, *Elements of Reform* (London, [1809]) p. 8.

25. Reprinted in T.B. Howell and T.J. Howell (eds), *A Complete Collection of State Trials* (London: Hansard, 1809-1828), xxiii, cols 154-160. It was also widely reported in the Irish press: see, *Dublin Evening Post,* 6 December 1792.

26. RH 2/4/66, SRO; the moderate William Morthland's original protest against 'the Irish paper' is in JC 26/280, SRO.

27. M. McTier to W. Drennan, 8 December 1792, no.356, Drennan Letters, T.765, PRONI.

28. L.M. Cullen, 'The internal politics of the United Irishmen', in D. Dickson, D. Keogh and K. Whelan (eds), *The United Irishmen: Republicanism, Radicalism and Rebellion* (Dublin: Lilliput, 1993) pp. 181-188.

29. *Northern Star*, 24-28 December 1792. The paper nevertheless printed the address, with many of the proprietors declaring it to be 'one of the finest papers [that] ever was written': M. McTier to W. Drennan, 8 December 1792, no. 356, Drennan Letters, T. 765, PRONI.

30. J. Brims, 'The Scottish Democratic Movement in the age of the French Revolution', unpublished PhD thesis, University of Edinburgh, 1993, p. 269.

31. Arniston MSS., RH 4/15/4, SRO.

32. McFarland, *Ireland and Scotland*, pp. 87-88.

33. Howell and Howell (eds), *State Trials*, xxiii, col. 224.

34. JC 26/280, SRO.

35. ibid.

36. Original of resolution in JC 26/289/31, SRO; see also coverage in *Edinburgh Gazetteer*, 3 December 1793.

37. Rebellion Papers 620/20/78, NAI.

38. Rebellion Papers 620/21/27, NAI.

39. Elliott, *Partners in Revolution*, p. xv.

40. Rebellion Papers 620/27/1, NAI.

41. Their hesitance was perhaps due to the torpor of events in Scotland during 1795, but may also have been due to doubts over their agent's suitability. He was James Tytler, the polymath Scottish radical and pioneer balloonist, who had fled Scotland for Belfast in January 1794 and whom the poet Burns described as 'an obscure, tippling though extraordinary body'.

42. Rebellion Papers 620/27/1, Smith/Bird information, NAI.

43. Newell's Report 21 July 1796, HO 100/62/141, Public Record Office; Frazier MSS. II 23, NAI.

44. ibid.

45. Rebellion Papers 620/35/130, A. Newton's information, 9 February 1798, NAI.

46. *Report from the Second Committee Enquiring into the Condition of the Poorer Classes in Ireland*. 1836 (40) XXXIV, p. 456.

47. ibid., p. 147; Minutes of the Hibernian Society 1792-1824, TD 200.7, Strathclyde Regional Archives (SRA).

48. J.E. Handley, *The Irish in Scotland, 1798-1845* (Cork: Cork University Press, 1943) p. 133.

49. Earl of Eglinton to R. Dundas, 12 March 1797, Laing MSS. II 500, University of Edinburgh.

50. In Coleraine the leaders of the local United Irishmen were being arrested, and 'their associates either dragged to prison or having to fly and leave their families and properties to the risk of danger': John Galt's Diary, 31 May 1797, D. 561, PRONI. The cheapest passage was on 'Bye Boats', carrying goods, livestock and passengers, and costing only 6d or 9d: Report of the Sheriff of Wigtown, RH 2/4/80 f.124, SRO.

51. Lord Grenville to Lord Pelham, 15 June 1797, Rebellion Papers 620/31/96, NAI; Earl of Galloway to R Dundas, 16 June 1797, RH 2/4/80 f.110, SRO; R. Dundas to J. King, 9 May 1797 RH 2/4/80 f.67, SRO.

52. R. Dundas to Duke of Portland, 13 January 1798, RH 2/4/83 f.21, SRO: he noted 'how exactly' they had copied United Irish proceedings.

53. R. Dundas to J. King, 18 April 1798, RH 2/4/83 f.170, SRO.

54. See, *Narrative of the Arrest, Examination and Imprisonment of George Mealmaker*, RH 2/4/83 ff.41-49, SRO.

55. McFarland, *Ireland and Scotland*, pp. 210-215.

56. T. Bartlett, 'An end to the Moral Economy: the Irish militia disturbances, 1793', *Past and Present*, no. 99, 1983, p. 58.

57. W.T.W. Tone (ed.), *Life of Theobald Wolfe Tone...* (Washington: Gales and Seaton, 1826) vol. 2, p. 432.

58. Compare the Dublin radical paper *The Press* which proclaimed on 3 February 1798: 'The United business in Scotland has increased to such a height as to attract the attention of the government in no small degree... There is talk of the United Scotsmen being FORTY THOUSAND in number ...'

59. McFarland, *Ireland and Scotland*, pp. 194-195.

60. *Glasgow Advertiser*, 15 January 1798. These were the Aberdeen Fencibles, the First and Second Battalions the Breadalbane Fencibles, the Reay Fencibles, the Loyal Tay Fencibles, the Second Battalion the Argyllshire Fencibles, the Caithness Legion, Frazier's Fencibles, Lord Elgin's Fifeshire Fencibles, the Inverness Highlanders, the North Lowland Regiment, the Perthshire Fencibles, the Ross-shire and Caithness Fencibles, and the Dunbartonshire Fencibles.

61. Frazier MSS. II 24, NAI.

62. Brims, 'The Scottish Democratic Movement', vol. 2, p. 573.

63. At the large open air meetings of 1819, for example, the crowd carried banners with the legend:
    Rose, Thistle and Shamrock blended,
    May the Rose of England never blow,
    May the Thistle of Scotland never grow,
    May the Harp of Ireland never play,
    Till Hunt, the Champion, wins the day.
    Spirit of the Union, 30 October 1819.

64. *Glasgow Herald*, 15 March 1813.

65. *Glasgow Chronicle*, 13 February 1816.

66. A. Colquhoun to Lord Sidmouth, 4 December 1812, RH 2/4/98 f.330, SRO.

67. *Glasgow Herald*, 15 March 1813. The Hibernian Society in Glasgow's East End was one of a variety of groups which contributed to their strike fund. The Society loaned £15 to the strikers. This may be the payment referred to in Minutes of the Hibernian Society, 24 and 25 November 1812, TD 200.7, SRA.

68. A. Maconochie to Lord Sidmouth, 25 December 1816, RH 2/4/112 f.729, SRO. The Spencean Philanthropists were also reported to have a Glasgow outpost: *Glasgow Chronicle*, 22 December 1817; *Hansard XXXV*, cols 411-418.

69. A.B. Richmond, *A Narrative of the Condition of the Manufacturing Population and the Proceedings of the Government which led to the State Trials in Scotland*, (Glasgow, [1824]) p. 183.

70. Lord Advocate's Precognitions, AD 14/17/18, SRO.

71. A. Machonochie to Lord Sidmouth, 26 December 1816, RH 2/4/112 f.722, SRO. McKinlay's position was possibly assisted by the receipt of a letter from Dublin which assured the Scots that they were backed by thousands in Ireland 'who were ready to go all lengths to the cause': A. Machonochie to Lord Sidmouth, 25 December 1816, RH 2/4/112 f.729, SRO.

72. A. Machonochie to Lord Sidmouth, 26 December 1816, RH 2/4/112 f.722, SRO.

73. C. Hope to Lord Pelham, 4 August 1803, RH 2/4/88 f.231, SRO. Note, for example, the Duke of Hamilton's comments on Lanarkshire which was: '… unfortunately surrounded by idle Irishmen, weavers and colliers, who created a general uneasiness; and if any means were to be carried into effect to separate the good from the bad, or to maintain order and public justice, it is required that the civil power and the peaceable part of the population should know how and where to find support and protection': *Glasgow Chronicle*, 9 December 1819.
74. See, *Glasgow Courier*, 29 March and 29 May 1798.

SCOTLAND AND ULSTER:
POLITICAL INTERACTIONS SINCE THE LATE NINETEENTH
CENTURY AND POSSIBILITIES OF CONTEMPORARY
DIALOGUE

Graham Walker

In this paper I would like to examine three aspects of the recent political relationship between Scotland and Ulster. First I want to explore the significance of that relationship at the time that Irish Home Rule emerged as an issue in British politics. This 'Home Rule era' – if I might so describe the period encompassing the three Irish Home Rule bills from the mid-1880s until the outbreak of the Great War – reveals a great deal about the Scottish influences on the Ulster unionist movement's opposition to Home Rule and about the extent of sympathy and support in Scotland for the unionist cause. It is a period in which the strength of the cultural bonds between the two places was nonetheless tempered by distinctive political values and priorities; and it is thus a period which reveals the modern complexities of the relationship between the two places.

Next, I want to proceed to a discussion of the extent to which Scotland continued to echo, politically and culturally, the experience of Ulster, even in the fundamentally distinct political contexts in which the two found themselves after 1921 following the creation of the Northern Ireland state. Finally, I want to offer some observations on the contemporary relationship between Scotland and Northern Ireland, with particular reference to the way in which the debate over possible constitutional change pulls both places together.

The Ulster-Scot enterprise

An interesting feature of the Ulster unionist reaction to the claims of Irish nationalism in this 'Home Rule era' is the extent to which, among Ulster Protestants, a distinctive ethnic identity is promoted, an identity which draws on the historic, religious and cultural bonds

The 'Ulster Scot', a postcard from the Home Rule era: a striking example of Ulster Unionists' assertion of historic, religious and cultural bonds with Scotland. Courtesy of the Ulster Museum.

with Scotland and which celebrates the 'Ulster-Scots' as a special people.[1]

In 1888, significantly soon after Gladstone had taken up the gauntlet of Irish Home Rule in 1886, a book entitled *The Scot in Ulster* was published in Edinburgh. Its author, John Harrison, was himself a Scot who was moved to write the work after visiting Ulster and being impressed by its Scottish characteristics. In the book he praised the 'Ulster Scots' as a resilient and resourceful people and he endorsed their fight against government from Dublin. He wrote:

> Time will help to bridge over the deep chasm which separates the Scot and the Irish in Ireland; but the cleavage is more likely to be closed if they both continue to live in the full communion of that great empire in which both may well glory.[2]

Harrison's work celebrated both an Ulster ethnic distinctiveness – in effect Protestant and heavily orientated to the Presbyterian and Scottish aspects of Ulster's heritage – and also a concept of the expansiveness of the Union and the Empire and their capacity to accommodate ethnic, racial and religious differences. These two themes – a form of ethnic exclusivism, and a more 'secular', all-encompassing pluralist unionism – have remained the central themes in Ulster unionism ever since. Yet the relationship between them has always been ambiguous and uneasy.

Harrison's was not an isolated work. In the late nineteenth- and early twentieth-century period there were several books which, albeit in different ways and with varying degrees of scholarliness, sought to promote the 'Ulster-Scot' enterprise. Such books included the prominent Presbyterian historian W.T. Latimer's *The Ulster Scot: his Faith and Fortune* (1899); the Presbyterian minister J.B. Woodburn's *The Ulster Scot: his History and Religion* (1914); and a number of other works which celebrated the heroic pioneering deeds of Ulster immigrants – Scots-born or descended from Scots – in America. Perhaps the best known of these works was Charles Hanna's two-volume *The Scotch-Irish* (1902), the 'Scotch-Irish' being the term for the 'Ulster-Scots' which was popularised in the USA.

The emergence of the Ulster-Scot industry in this period was largely in response to Irish nationalist assumptions about the ethnic homogeneity of the Irish. Ulster unionists sought to disrupt the coherence and easy fluency of the Irish nationalist view of Ireland as a nation, one and indivisible, with an historic destiny to be self-

governing. Unionists were in effect acknowledging that their protes-
tations of loyalty to the Union, as Irishmen, were not enough: their
case against Irish nationalism was felt to be strengthened by the insistence that there were two Irelands – at least – each with its own
claims and aspirations and each with the testimonials of historical
struggle to accompany them. Thus, within the unionist movement in
Ireland, there were, to use current terminology, both 'civic' and 'ethnic' strains of argument. There was, first, the argument which promoted the Union as beneficial to the whole of Ireland, regardless of
who you were or where you came from; and there was, then, the argument that Ulster Protestants – and it had to be *Ulster* given their
concentration there – formed a distinctive people with their own
rights in opposition to those of Irish Catholics.

For our purposes, I think it should be noted how particularly
Scottish and Presbyterian this cultivation of an 'Ulster' ethnic identity
proved to be. Perhaps, as epitomised by Woodburn's book, *The Ulster
Scot*, Presbyterianism became in effect the religious identity of Ulster
Protestantism. The actual denominational divisions and intra-
Presbyterian struggles of Ulster's Protestant history were largely
elided in the cause of constructing a coherent 'passion play' which
would answer the Irish Catholic story with the Ulster-Scot epic: both
resonated with the themes of sacrifice, suffering and heroic struggle.
In a sense, Woodburn's tome crowned the whole enterprise conducted by certain unionists in the Home Rule era: that of controvert-
ing the unitary vision of Irish nationalism by counterposing an
alternative ethnic origin-myth and an alternative interpretation of
Irish history. The Ulster-Scots were presented as a people who were
the very stuff of the British Empire's civilising mission, the 'cutting
edge' or 'advance guard' of Empire.

Perhaps the most interesting members of the unionist leadership
to promote such notions were Presbyterian Liberal Unionists such as
T.W. Russell, who had been born in Scotland, and Thomas Sinclair,
who made much of his Scottish Covenanter origins. The significance
of men like Russell and Sinclair was that they came from a liberal
political background, that they were typical of the anti-established
Church, Presbyterian, Dissenting tradition which was a potent political force in Ulster, at least until the advent of Irish Home Rule.
Confident in their belief that Home Rule would mean a Roman
Catholic ascendancy throughout the whole of Ireland, and fearing
for the position of Presbyterians who had had to endure second-class
status under an Anglican ascendancy for so long, Liberals such as

Russell and Sinclair felt betrayed by Gladstone and broke with the Liberal Party on the issue of Home Rule. An Ulster Liberal Unionist Association was formed and it was to play an important role in the wider unionist campaigns against successive Home Rule bills in 1886, 1893 and 1912.[3]

Much was invested by these Presbyterian anti-Home Rulers in the hope that support for their cause would be generated among their fellow-Presbyterians in Scotland. The nature of the appeals for support that were made to Scotland were revealing of the strength of Ulster-Scottish bonds, at least in the minds of those in Ulster. In 1886, in a speech at Grangemouth in Stirlingshire, T.W. Russell exhorted his audience to respond to their ethnic duties as he clearly viewed them. He said:

Three hundred years ago Ulster was peopled by Scotch settlers for State reasons. You are bound to remember this. The men are bone of your bone, flesh of your flesh. The blood of the Covenanters courses through their veins; they read the same Bible, they sing the same Psalms, they have the same Church polity.[4]

Thomas Sinclair is widely held to have been responsible for drawing up the Ulster Covenant of 1912 by which unionists, in their hundreds of thousands, pledged to resist Home Rule.[5] The Covenant took its inspiration from the Scottish model of the 1640s; and this episode is in many ways typical of the way in which the unionist struggle was identified with the language and imagery of an essentially Scottish cultural heritage. Ulster's fight against Home Rule took on the Covenanting character of Presbyterian struggles of old. Moreover, there occurred, in February 1912, a large Presbyterian anti-Home Rule Convention at which resolutions and speeches explicitly affirming Scottish cultural identity and inspiration were delivered.[6]

This whole process rather obscured those components in unionism which were English rather than Scottish in origin. The Orange Order to some extent gave expression to these English elements but, nevertheless, it might be argued that the Solemn League and Covenant, events such as the Presbyterian Convention of 1912, and the appearance of historical works such as Woodburn's constitute something of a 'hi-jack' of the unionist cause by a tradition popularly known by this time as that of the 'Ulster Scot'. This is perhaps not so surprising when it is remembered that the Presbyterian tradition was

Ulster's
Solemn League and Covenant.

Being convinced in our consciences that Home Rule would be disastrous to the material well-being of Ulster as well as of the whole of Ireland, subversive of our civil and religious freedom, destructive of our citizenship and perilous to the unity of the Empire, we, whose names are underwritten, men of Ulster, loyal subjects of His Gracious Majesty King George V., humbly relying on the God whom our fathers in days of stress and trial confidently trusted, do hereby pledge ourselves in solemn Covenant throughout this our time of threatened calamity to stand by one another in defending for ourselves and our children our cherished position of equal citizenship in the United Kingdom and in using all means which may be found necessary to defeat the present conspiracy to set up a Home Rule Parliament in Ireland. ¶ And in the event of such a Parliament being forced upon us we further solemnly and mutually pledge ourselves to refuse to recognise its authority. ¶ In sure confidence that God will defend the right we hereto subscribe our names. ¶ And further, we individually declare that we have not already signed this Covenant.

The above was signed by me at_____
"Ulster Day," Saturday, 28th September, 1912.

_____

——— God Save the King. ———

The Ulster Solemn League and Covenant, 1912, a further example of Ulster Unionism drawing on the imagery of a Scottish cultural heritage.

better geared to the rebelliousness which loyalists displayed from 1912 to 1914, at least in relation to the government of the day.

The nature of solidarity with Ulster

The promotion of the Ulster-Scot enterprise was a response to Irish nationalist ideology; but it was also a politically expedient means of attempting to influence opinion in Britain, and particularly in Scotland, over Home Rule. As has been noted, Ulster unionists made strenuous efforts to play up the 'kith and kin' theme in Scotland. Their success in this regard, however, was limited.

It appears to be the case that just as it was Liberal Unionists who were, largely, the most enthusiastic proponents of an Ulster identity, which drew so heavily on its Scottish dimensions, so, in Scotland, it was Liberal Unionists who responded most positively. One obvious connecting theme here was economics: this shared view was in many ways a show of solidarity between the industrial, commercial and business elites of the west of Scotland and north-east Ulster. The social and economic character of both areas lent itself to intense regional pride and to a sense of great self-importance, centred around notions of progress and prosperity. It was also, of course, about economic self-interest: both sets of industrialists and traders feared what they took to be the baleful implications of a Dublin parliament for the industrial and commercial interests of their regions. The Glasgow Chamber of Commerce even considered that a Home Rule Ireland would be a haven for hostile foreign armies and a grave threat to Britain's security. The argument that Irish Home Rule would strike at the integrity of the Empire was one which signally bound the Clyde and the Lagan Valley: this era marked the high tide of popular regard in both places for the Empire, that is, for the Empire as the guarantee of social and economic progress. And in both places the economic elites tended to be Liberal Unionists, fearful of radicalism but often contemptuous of the Conservatism of the rural landed aristocracy.

Both sets of Liberal Unionists, fired by Whiggish beliefs in imperial progressiveness, were probably the most enthusiastic adherents of *British* identity in the UK as a whole. The Ulster unionist attempts to foster and strengthen the notion of British solidarity found their most positive response in urban west-central Scotland, both among Liberal Unionist business circles and a working class influenced by the Orange Order. The Ulster cause prompted its Scottish supporters to move some way towards incorporating their Scottish national identity in a British variant. In 1895 Thomas Sinclair could feel confident enough of his Glasgow audience's feelings of national identity to draw the following Scottish parallel with the proposed rule of Ulster from Dublin:

> It is just as if it were proposed to transfer the interests of ship-builders and manufacturers of Glasgow from Imperial Parliament to the control of a legislature swamped by the crofters of the Highlands.[7]

To some extent the Liberal Unionists of west-central Scotland might be said to have 'bought in' to the Ulster-Scot enterprise which was being promoted in Ulster from the 1880s. A Liberal Unionist in all but name by the time he made the following remark in 1912, Lord Rosebery might be taken as representative of this tendency. He said:

> I love Highlanders and I love Lowlanders, but when I come to the branch of our race which has been grafted on to the Ulster stem I take off my hat with veneration and awe. They are, I believe, without exception the toughest, the most dominant, the most irresistible race that exists in the universe at this moment.[8]

The Liberal Unionists in Scotland were prone to portray the Ulster cause in terms every bit as apocalyptic as those used in Ulster itself. In 1912, when the Liberal Unionists and the Conservatives in Scotland were on the point of merger into what would become known as the 'Scottish Unionist Party', the following eulogy and message of support to the Ulster unionists was minuted in the final meeting of the West of Scotland Liberal Unionist Association:

> In Ulster the fight is hottest. The finest population in Ireland are being driven to extremes, and are imploring our help. They believe that their rights as British citizens, the peace of their homes, the prosperity of their businesses, their religious freedom itself, are all involved in the struggle. No Scotsman could read without deep emotion the narrative of a vast and loyal population, closely united to us by ties of race and religion, flocking to their churches to implore the most High to avert the threatened danger, and we in the West of Scotland, of all in the British Isles, should hold out a strong hand to them in their hour of distress.[9]

The 'narrative' referred to is likely to have been understood largely as the stirring and heroic saga of the Ulster-Scots seeking moral and indeed practical support from their spiritual homeland. And, contrary to what is sometimes suggested, there was a significant rallying of Scottish support for the Ulster unionists during the Home Rule crisis of 1912-1914. This is evidenced by large public meetings and demonstrations, by Covenant signings, by feverishly pro-Ulster newspaper editorials, and by motions of support passed at specially convened meetings of Church presbyteries.

Yet the merger of the Liberal Unionists with the Conservatives in 1912 probably had the effect, in time, of somewhat damping down the campaign for solidarity with Ulster. Certainly, in terms of the expression of such a campaign through a heightened enthusiasm for British national identity, it can be argued that the Conservative influence was, if anything, a restraining one. As Richard Finlay has argued, the Conservatives in Scotland were much more circumspect about 'the ditching of Scottish nationality in order to achieve British homogeneity'.[10] They were, of course, impeccably loyalist and pro-British; but they were acutely aware of the sensitivities surrounding issues of nationalism and national identity, and of the depth of Scottish national feeling and the potential resentments which might be aroused by attempts to absorb it or to marginalise it. The Conservatives also appeared better aware of how Scotland's participation in the Empire had intensified both Scottish identity and a Scottish sense of competitiveness vis-a-vis England. A Scottish Unionist Party memorandum in 1914 stressed the sensitive nature of the Scottish national question; it urged party candidates to try to direct Scottish national feelings to the ends of the Empire, and counselled them to use the argument that Scottish Home Rule would close off avenues of career advancement for ambitious Scots in *England*.[11] After the merger of 1912, the Unionists, if anything, prioritised issues concerning Scottish nationality above the issue of Ulster, and this became ever more evident as the Irish constitutional question in general departed the political scene after 1922.

With a wider geographical base than that of the Liberal Unionists, the Conservatives also knew to their cost just how deeply entrenched were the traditionally Liberal, and often radical, political attitudes of small-town and rural Scotland, steeped as they were in bitter quarrels over land and over the issues of patronage and disestablishment which had riven the Church of Scotland. Ulster unionists made a very limited impact on these particular Scottish fellow-Presbyterians who felt that they could not, in any circumstances, align themselves with the Conservatives as the Liberal Unionists had done. The Conservatives, in short, were more cognisant of the wider Scottish and, indeed, British political contexts and were less willing than the Liberal Unionists to subordinate other political priorities to the cause of Ulster, strongly though they supported the loyalists' position. In contrast to the Liberal Unionists, the Conservatives were more than simply a reflection of the west of Scotland urban-industrial ethos. Moreover, it was Scottish Conservatives such as Frederick Scott Oliver who, in the early twentieth century, were among those advocating 'Home Rule All Round' or 'federal' schemes of constitutional reform for the UK, schemes to which Liberal Unionists were hostile or, at best, cool. It was largely the Conservatives, a numerical majority in the new Scottish Unionist Party after 1912, who ensured that the party would be guided on Ulster, as on other issues, by pragmatic political calculation rather than by emotive 'soulbrother' rhetoric. Scottish unionists in general had always exuded more self-confidence and held more expansive political visions than had Ulster unionists; the latter, preoccupied with the quest for security from the threat of Dublin rule, were always distinguished by a defensive, and ultimately narrow and exclusivist, approach to British and imperial identity.[12]

The position after 1920

With the establishment of devolved government for the new six-county Northern Ireland under the terms of the Government of Ireland Act of 1920, the political contexts of Scotland and Ulster diverged fundamentally. Ulster now really was 'a place apart' inasmuch as it was the only part of the UK to have its own devolved legislature and its own ethnically-based party system, distinct from that of Britain. Scotland, on the other hand, was integrated even more fully, after the First World War, into the adversarial politics of Westminster which, increasingly, meant the two-party, class-based struggle between Conservatives and Labour.

It is therefore necessary to stress the divergences between Scotland and Northern Ireland, politically speaking, which resulted from the contrasting constitutional positions which characterised them after 1921. Nevertheless, significant echoes of the religious and political divisions of Northern Ireland continued to be heard in Scotland; and there are many points which can be made both about the prevalence of Ulster or Irish political overtones and about the limits to their influence. This is what I want to explore now.

Let us take, firstly, the inter-war period. Until scholars such as Tom Gallagher and Steve Bruce started to highlight the religious tensions of inter-war Scotland, the historiography of this period had been concerned largely with images of working-class solidarity and political radicalism: religious conflict was seen merely as a minor modification of the dominant picture of class unity. However, it is now clear that, to a large extent, strong class and religious group loyalties co-existed and, I would suggest, even fed off each other in certain circumstances.

The 'Orange versus Green' rivalry in Scotland in many ways pre-served its original, Irish character. Elaine McFarland's work on Orangeism in Scotland in the nineteenth century shows clearly that the Orange Order was primarily a movement of Protestant Irish immigrants – overwhelmingly, of course, from Ulster – into Scotland in that century.[13] I would go further and suggest that the Order continued to draw heavily on the descendants of this commu-nity well into the twentieth century and that the terms of the Orange-Green conflict in Scotland, at least until the Second World War, were redolent of Irish conditions. Put simply, the Protestant immigrants brought with them to Scotland their fears about Catholic aggression and what political scientists like to call a 'zero-sum game' mentality: that is, that when Catholics improved their position it had to be at the expense of Protestants. In Scotland the Protestant Irish looked around and found their old foe – the Catholic Irish – in sizeable and seemingly ever-increasing numbers, 'manoeuvring' themselves, as they saw it, into positions of power. The Catholics, for their part, saw in the Orange processions the kind of triumphalism which they or their ancestors had faced in Ulster. The essential nature of the conflict in Ireland was thus to a great extent transplanted. In inter-war Scotland, in times of economic depression and political flux, the Orange outlook came to be more widely shared and was taken up by the Presbyterian Churches to further their own role as supposed guardians of the 'national interest'. The Churches, and much other influential opinion in Scotland, were deeply anxious about what they saw as the effects of a large Irish Catholic presence when set against the background of high emigration from Scotland. In the 1920s about 400,000 Scots emigrated, mostly to Commonwealth countries such as Canada.

The Unionists (Conservatives) in Scotland made use, at local level, of an essentially Ulster or Irish political language – what I would call 'the language of loyalism' – which held that loyalty to the state, and to the Crown, should be rewarded, for example with jobs, and that 'disloyalty' in this regard should not be rewarded. It was by using such language that the Unionists could continue to appeal, in a populist fashion, to Protestants and to combat the political threat of Protestant extremist organisations like Alexander Ratcliffe's Scottish Protestant League, a significant force in local politics in Glasgow in the 1930s.[14]

However, as the sociologist Steve Bruce has pointed out,[15] the Unionists in Scotland, in contrast to the Unionists in Northern Ireland, had no 'pork barrel' from which to reward working-class supporters and, ultimately, were part of a political party whose wider, British agenda offered little scope for religious sectarianism. Special pleading on issues such as Irish Catholic immigration into Scotland made little headway in the Conservative Party as a whole because action on such issues would have been contrary to the Party's desire to make a broad appeal across class and religious divisions in Britain as a whole.

The Unionist hold on the Protestant working class in Scotland was thus in no way nearly as tight as it was in Northern Ireland where, incidentally, it was also subject to extremist challenge. In addition, I would make the point that two important issues on which the Orange Order concentrated and rallied support – namely the 1918 Education Act and mixed marriages – did not break down into neat and tidy political terms. After all, it was the Conservative-dominated coalition government that passed the 1918 Act, which provided for full state support for Catholic Schools in Scotland, and it was a Conservative government that passed the Catholic Relief Act in 1926. The latter allowed the Orange Order to claim that the state was strengthening the position of the Catholic Church while the Church itself was attempting to undermine the law of the land with its stance on mixed marriages: in 1908 the Roman Catholic Church had issued a decree, *Ne Temere*, which held that mixed marriages not sanctified by the rites of their Church were invalid and that all children of mixed marriages were to be brought up as Catholics. This decree outraged Protestant opinion in Ulster as well as Scotland. In Ulster it was a significant factor in fuelling unionist fears about the role of the Catholic Church in a Home Rule Ireland.

However, to return to the era following the First World War, the point I want to emphasise is that sectarian conflict in Scotland had, and indeed still has, its own logic and terms of reference. In Scotland, unlike Northern Ireland, these did not translate so straightforwardly into corresponding political divisions. If the Unionists were able to mobilise Protestant working-class opinion in certain key constituencies, this support was nonetheless limited nor was it all that reliable. Indeed, the inter-war period witnessed a lot of Unionist, Orange, and Presbyterian Church anxiety about the appeal of Labour politics and of socialist ideas to the Protestant working class. Valuable as Catholic working-class support was to Labour after 1918, it required even more Protestant working-class support to attain the electoral breakthrough of 1922 and to sustain Labour – which in the 1920s and early 1930s was, in effect, the Independent Labour Party – as the force it became thereafter.

I have alluded to a Catholic-Labour alliance. This was forged in the years following the First World War and is often presumed to have been based solely on Labour's willingness to support the 1918 Education Act and the rights of Catholic schools. Recently, however, the historian John McCaffrey has published an article which broadens the analysis of this alliance beyond the issue of education alone.[16] McCaffrey argues cogently that wider social issues were of greater importance in Labour's appeal to Catholics and, furthermore, that the Catholic Church itself did not rush to secure Labour's backing: quite the contrary, for it was by no means obvious in 1918 and the years immediately following it that Labour would turn out to be the political force it did. McCaffrey's revisionist work is helpful for it encourages us to look beyond a simple 'Labour-Catholic pact' on education. It seems that Labour made a successful appeal on issues like housing, which transcended sectarian loyalties, and that both Protestant and Catholic workers identified Labour primarily with such issues. As a result of McCaffrey's work we can also make sense of the Scottish National Party's recent development as a party also concerned with social issues. Indeed the continuing attachment of Catholics to Labour down the years might in part be explained by the failure of rival political parties to take a sufficiently strong stance on social issues. The electoral need to win Catholic support away from Labour has thus helped to mould the SNP in recent times into more of a social movement, articulating a wide range of social concerns as well as the nationalist agenda. It should also be noted at this point that Catholic suspicion that an independent or Home Rule Scotland would be 'another Stormont' – with Protestants discriminating against Catholics – induced Labour to drop its commitment to Scottish Home Rule between the late 1920s and the early 1970s, and has also made the SNP's task of attracting Catholic support very difficult right up until the present day.[17]

Let me turn now to the era following the Second World War. The main feature of Scottish politics since the war has been the decline of the Unionists, a decline which has been most notable in areas where the Protestant working-class vote was most significant. It should be said that this decline has not been sudden or strictly continuous. The Unionists, for example, recorded their most impressive electoral performance in 1955, winning over half of the total Scottish vote. In the mid-1960s, survey evidence suggested that there was still a relatively strong correlation between religion and politics in Scotland, with the comparatively high Protestant working-class Unionist vote and the solidly Catholic Labour vote its most salient features. It is from this point, in the mid-1960s, I suggest, that the situation began to change most rapidly, with two factors of particular importance.

The first is the end of the Empire and with it the appeal of Empire loyalism, although it can be strongly argued that the end of Empire did not in itself automatically mean a decline in the political significance of the idea of Britishness. However, the decline of Empire did adversely affect the ability of the Unionists to strike a populist note in Scotland, an ability further adversely affected, it is generally agreed, by the decision in 1965 to dissolve the distinctive identity of the Scottish Unionist Party by changing its name officially to 'Conservative'.

The second factor is that of secularisation, a factor emphasised in the work of Steve Bruce. Bruce has commented on the way in which Scotland diverged from the more religiously orientated society of Northern Ireland where such variables as church attendance, opinions on moral issues, sabbatarianism and so on all characterised a society defying wider secular trends. Scotland, by contrast, was largely in line with trends in the rest of Britain. Along with secularisation went factors such as demographic change, which disrupted the political and religious character of communities; more inter-marriage; and better ecumenical relations between the Churches. Catholics largely ceased to be regarded as a threatening presence, and concepts of Scottish identity and nationality came to be more truly shared.[18]

The contemporary situation

With the outbreak of the Troubles in Northern Ireland in 1969 it was widely feared that Scotland could be plunged into similar turmoil. This has not happened. The political effects of the Northern Ireland situation have been limited and well contained. Scots, in general, have reacted to the horrors of Northern Ireland with a determination to prevent an overspill. Electorally, however, the most obvious effect of developments in Northern Ireland has been to damage the Conservatives. For example, the Heath government's prorogation of the Stormont Parliament in 1972 seems to have been one factor in what was a disproportionately Protestant 'protest vote' for the SNP in the two general elections of 1974. Moreover, in 1987, the Tories were, to a limited extent, harmed by protests over the signing of the Anglo-Irish Agreement of 1985 and by the formation, by disaffected members of the Orange Order, of the short-lived and significantly named 'Scottish Unionist Party'.

Conservatives and Unionists in Scotland in the 1990s have not generally sought to exploit the Northern Ireland issue in order to arrest their party's electoral decline or to win back former constituencies of support in the Protestant community. It seems very unlikely that a traditional, unionist approach to the issue would reap any electoral dividends in the contemporary Scottish political climate with its restless mood in relation to matters of constitutional reform.

Perhaps, more importantly, the spectre of sectarian conflict in Scotland has engendered a deep wariness in all political parties about being identified, in one way or the other, with the Northern Ireland situation. Such caution has, if anything, become further entrenched since the Monklands by-election of 1994. The background to this may be briefly sketched. For some two years before the by-election there had been controversy over the way in which Monklands District Council in Lanarkshire had been conducting its affairs. The Council was controlled by the local Labour Party which was overwhelmingly Catholic in composition. Among the issues raised were allegations that the Council had been operating a deliberate policy of investing in areas of predominantly Catholic population in the District at the expense of Protestant ones, and of preferring Catholics to Protestants for local employment. At the by-election in 1994, caused by the death of the Labour Party leader John Smith, much evidence of religious tensions came to the fore and sounded a warning that, in contemporary Scotland, such divisions in society had not become as insignificant as many commentators had believed. In the aftermath of the election these same commentators began to speculate about the possibility of Scotland becoming 'another Northern Ireland' in the event of independence.[19]

The effect of the Monklands episode has probably been to further inhibit Scottish contributions to the debate about Northern Ireland.

This is a great pity, because I would suggest that the debate has been impoverished by the relative absence of a distinctive Scottish voice. Notwithstanding understandable worries about the exacerbation of religious divisions in Scotland, I think it is important that Scots should engage in a meaningful dialogue with the people of Northern Ireland. This dialogue could be far-reaching. It might, for example, be particularly helpful to the unionist or loyalist community in Northern Ireland. I say this because I believe that the loyalists need to be heard more clearly and need to be prevented from turning inwards and allowing their resentments to fester.

For a long time now loyalists have drawn attention to the disadvantage they experience when they compare, on the one hand, the wider hinterland of support for the nationalist cause in the Republic of Ireland, and indeed abroad, and, on the other, the relative absence of support for the unionist position in Britain. Furthermore, they contrast the influential role played by the Republic in discussions of Northern Ireland affairs with the self-proclaimed neutrality of the British government. This perception of imbalance is at the heart of loyalist insecurity and fears. Nationalists have never quite grasped that, as long as such insecurity and fears are fuelled, loyalists will be likely to pull down the shutters on matters of all-Ireland co-operation and, indeed, of a shared Irish identity. Progress in these matters will be more likely to occur if loyalists can feel they are being encouraged and given the space to develop stronger links with Britain. Only then, with their desire to strengthen the Union acknowledged, might they relax sufficiently to consider the benefits of Irish dimensions. This is where Scotland can contribute.

Loyalists in general feel better able to communicate with Scots. They think that they receive a more sympathetic hearing in Scotland. Now, it may in fact be the case that fewer Scots these days are prepared to extend such sympathy. Scotland is a society which has changed profoundly in recent years: it is much more pluralistic, it is decidedly less inclined to accept the label 'British', and it is no longer a 'Protestant country' in the way it undoubtedly once was. All of this will be uncomfortable, if not unpalatable, to some Ulster unionists.

Nevertheless, it remains important that unionists/loyalists are encouraged to articulate their feelings: their sense of cultural identity, their affinities with Scotland, their interpretation of history, and their aspirations regarding future political developments. Scots might still play an important role by engaging in a dialogue on these issues.

And it could be a genuine dialogue. It need not only be predominantly one-way. Scotland itself has a lot to gain from such a dialogue in relation to its own social, religious and cultural divisions and its own political and constitutional aspirations. In the debate about Scottish devolution much of value can still be gleaned from Northern Ireland's actual experience of devolved government between 1921 and 1972, and from the fact that the province has been used as something of a 'constitutional laboratory' for different schemes of devolution and power-sharing ever since. For the present at least, constitutional changes affecting one part of the UK will have considerable ramifications for the other parts, and it is arguably the case that Scotland and Northern Ireland – where the various demands for change and the debates about change are most intense – are the two places with most in common. The relationship of both Scotland and Northern Ireland to the state is central to the way in which the Union has developed historically and to the way in which it is currently struggling to work to the satisfaction of its constituent parts.

It is indeed a serious mistake to confine the Northern Ireland problem within a one-island framework. As Ian McBride argues, the Ulster problem is very much a British problem.[20] It is about the haphazard and in some ways artificial development of the UK. It is about the multi-definitional character of 'Britishness'. Britishness is not a single, homogeneous entity. Rather it represents a plurality of identities, some of which, like that of the Ulster loyalists, can seem, for example to the English, to be very 'unBritish', given the common English perception of what Britishness should mean. However, the Ulster loyalist sense of identity is far more understandable to Scots, whatever their views on the desirability of a united Ireland. Scots can sympathise with Ulster loyalist frustration regarding the English equation of 'English' with 'British'. Scots know very well about religious sectarianism and about a system of education segregated, in effect, according to religion. Scots can readily relate to the potency of Orange and Green symbolism. In such respects Scotland and Ulster are indeed close cousins. Potentially, they can do much together to deconstruct the concept of Britishness and perhaps to redefine it more beneficially for all. They might even cooperate productively towards the restructuring of the UK and help to strengthen the concept of the UK as a 'union state', encompassing and stimulating diversity, rather than as a 'unitary state', debilitatingly bound to a metropolitan centre. There may thus occur in the process a strengthening of regionalist ideas whose advocates in the past included the late John Hewitt, a figure who demands to be invoked in any discus-

sion of Scottish-Ulster relations. In short, Scotland and Northern
Ireland might press the argument, most tellingly, that two centralised
nation states do not adequately reflect the interactions within and
between these two islands. Even Scottish nationalists, who base much
of their case on the premise that the Union has meant cultural sub-
ordination or even absorption by a larger neighbour, might be
induced to appreciate that central to the Ulster loyalist case is the parallel fear that a united Ireland would, in the present circumstances,
bring about *their* cultural marginalisation.

A dialogue between Scotland and Ulster could thus be far-reaching. It would focus on the constitutional debate which bears down on
both places but it would go beyond this into matters of identity and
the co-existence of different identities. It could address ways of constructing pluralist identities for both Scotland and Northern Ireland
in opposition to ethnically purist and sectarian forces in both places.
By such forces I mean the dogmatic anti-Britishness of strands of Irish
nationalism and republicanism; the loyalist mirror-image of myopic
anti-Irishness; the problem for Scottish nationalism of proving that it
does not depend on a visceral anti-Englishness for its momentum;
and the matter of religious antagonisms in both Scotland and
Northern Ireland. It might encompass an agenda best described as
bolstering the 'civic' while deepening awareness of the tight grip still
exercised by the 'ethnic'.

NOTES

1. An expanded discussion of the theme of this section will be published in the
   near future: see, G. Walker and D. Officer, 'Scottish Unionism and Ulster' in
   D. Forsyth (ed.) *Unionist Scotland, 1800-1995* (Edinburgh: John Donald)
   forthcoming.
2. J. Harrison, *The Scot in Ulster* (Edinburgh: Blackwood, 1888) p.114.
3. See J.R. Fisher, *The Ulster Liberal Unionist Association: a Sketch of its History,
   1885-1914* (Belfast: Ulster Liberal Unionist Association, 1914).
4. Speech quoted in A.W. Samuels, *Home Rule: What is it?* (Dublin; London,
   1911).
5. For a discussion of Sinclair's career see G. Walker, 'Thomas Sinclair:
   Presbyterian Liberal Unionist' in R. English and G. Walker (eds) *Unionism in
   Modern Ireland: New Perspectives on Politics and Culture* (Basingstoke:
   Macmillan, 1996) pp. 19-40.
6. This event is discussed in G. Walker, *Intimate Strangers: Political and Cultural
   Interaction between Scotland and Ulster in Modern Times* (Edinburgh: John
   Donald, 1995) pp. 29-43.
7. *Northern Whig*, 9 March 1895.
8. This quotation was used by Woodburn for the frontispiece of his book *The
   Ulster Scot*.

9. Minute book of the West of Scotland Liberal Unionist Association, 5 December 1912, National Library of Scotland (NLS) Acc.10424/22.
10. R. Finlay, 'Imperial Scotland: Scottish national identity and the British Empire, c.1850-1914', unpublished paper delivered to the annual conference of the Association of Scottish Historical Studies, April 1994.
11. Bonar Law Papers, House of Lords Records Office 32/3/30.
12. For a fuller discussion of this theme see, Walker, *Intimate Strangers*, chap. 2, pp. 17-60.
13. E. McFarland, *'Protestants First!' The Orange Order in Scotland in the Nineteenth Century* (Edinburgh: Edinburgh University Press, 1991).
14. See, G. Walker, 'The Orange Order in Scotland between the Wars', *International Review of Social History*, vol. 37, 1992, pp. 177-206.
15. S. Bruce, 'Sectarianism in Scotland: a contemporary assessment and explanation', *Scottish Government Yearbook*, 1988, pp. 150-165.
16. J. McCaffrey, 'Irish issues in the nineteenth and twentieth century: radicalism in a Scottish context', in T.M. Devine (ed.) *Irish Immigrants and Scottish Society in the Nineteenth and Twentieth Centuries* (Edinburgh: John Donald, 1991) pp. 116-137.
17. See M. Dyer, 'Scotland: does Northern Ireland make a difference?', *Parliamentary Brief*, November 1994, pp. 84-85.
18. These are the conclusions reached by Tom Gallagher in his pioneering study *Glasgow: the Uneasy Peace* (Manchester: Manchester University Press, 1987).
19. The episode is discussed in Walker, *Intimate Strangers*, pp. 180-184.
20. I. McBride, 'Ulster and the British problem' in English and Walker (eds), *Unionism in Modern Ireland*, pp. 1-18.

LANGUAGE AND LITERATURE

THE NATURE OF THE ULSTER-SCOTS LANGUAGE COMMUNITY

Linde Lunney

Many of you will have heard, or will at least have heard of, the old-style Presbyterian sermons. I am modelling my discourse today on those old sermons: they seem an appropriate structure for a talk on an aspect of Ulster-Scots traditional culture. You will be relieved to hear that I do not plan to thunder at you for an hour and a half, but I will deal with my material under the proverbial 'three heads'; and I do have a text of sorts, but it is secular and, perversely, held back to the end of the talk.

The nature of the Ulster-Scots *language* community

My first heading places the emphasis on 'language'. I want to introduce to you two ways in which any language, and perhaps also any language community, can be studied: synchronically or diachronically.

If you opt for a synchronic approach, you look at the language situation at a given moment, analysing the social aspects of language use, the ways in which individual speakers select levels of formality suitable to different occasions; or perhaps you examine the variations in pronunciation between regions. This approach is possibly the more fashionable one today, partly because it is more amenable to the use of late twentieth-century technology: you can tape-record or video-record individual speakers, analyse the output instrumentally, do statistical analyses of occurrences, and plot variations on maps using computer programs and graphics.

A diachronic analysis looks at how a language changes through time: it was probably most popular with language scholars in the late eighteenth and nineteenth centuries, with their grounding in the classical languages of Greece and Rome. You can study how French developed from vulgar Latin, or how Shakespeare's vowel sounds differ from Chaucer's, or if there is any Pictish influence on Scots. Of course, in the absence of machine recording, the historical linguist has to rely on the written record, and decoding a sound system from the conventions of a written spelling system is notoriously difficult. Sometimes present-day variations must be analysed to shed light on how a language developed.

Let us turn to look at some aspects of the history of language in Ulster. I will set up a diachronic framework, and illustrate it with some synchronic snapshots of language in society at different historical periods. Ulster's links with Scottish languages predate by hundreds of years the seventeenth-century population movements of the Plantation before which Ulster was, like most of Ireland, largely Gaelic-speaking. The form of Gaelic found in Ulster was strongly influenced by the Scots Gaelic of the western seaboard of Scotland: the ruling families, and presumably the underclasses as well, moved easily between the two coasts – marrying and fighting being the main reasons for contact. The Gaelic of Rathlin Island was to all intents and purposes a dialect of Scots Gaelic, and present-day Ulster Irish shows features typical of Scots Gaelic.

This means that there is a very complex set of influences from the underlying Gaelic stratum at work on the English speech of Ulster. The speech of Tyrone and Fermanagh, derived at least in part from the speech of English settlers, is probably the most clearly influenced by Ulster – that is, Scots-influenced – Irish but there are Gaelic influences too on the Ulster-Scots dialect of Antrim and even Down. Ulster-Scots is a dialect of Scots which is itself a dialect of English as developed in Scotland and influenced by Scots Gaelic; so Ulster-Scots is, potentially at least, subject to influence from both Ulster Irish and Scots Gaelic.

It is always easier to spot and cite specific Gaelic vocabulary items, like 'moiley' for a hornless cow, from Gaelic *maol* (bald) than it is to study pronunciation and syntax; but dialectologists, such as the late Brendan Adams of the Ulster Folk Museum, have established quite an array of evidence and have even attempted to use material from Ulster-Scots and Ulster-English to elucidate problems in Irish Gaelic and Scots Gaelic dialectology.[1]

I have sometimes wondered how the linguistic situation in Ulster would have developed if the Plantation had brought over only the *English* settlers in the seventeenth century. Other parts of the world provide examples of what happens where two distinctive languages are in contact. Sometimes, as in Louisiana, a creole, which produces its own history and even literature, develops between them. Or sometimes the population as a whole tends to bilingualism, which may be either transient or permanent, as in Belgium. So much depends on the social context. At any rate, Ulster Irish in the seventeenth century could not hold its own against the two-pronged incursion of English and Scots. Brendan Adams has calculated that an area within a radius of twenty-five miles of Belfast was 99% English-speaking by at least 1760, no matter what language had been spoken there by previous generations; and he extrapolates back in time to about 1700 to suggest that Irish was, even at that date, in retreat over much of Antrim and Down.[2]

If we stop to look at the linguistic situation at the beginning of the eighteenth century we are, of course, guessing; but there must have been considerable linguistic confusion and problems of communication. Indeed, such difficulties would have been considerably exacerbated because both English dialects and Scots dialects were more strongly differentiated from each other than they are today. There was no recognised standard form of English until much later, so the speech of one of Sir Fulke Conway's men from Devon, but settled in south Antrim, would have been quite different from that of a Lancashire merchant living in Belfast; and officials from the east of Scotland would have had difficulty with the speech of Galloway men. To add to the mix, there would have been speakers of Ulster Irish and Scots Gaelic, rubbing shoulders with Scots and English settlers in the local fairs. Some of the early Presbyterian ministers were able, and perhaps had to be able, to preach in Irish, so the different groups may well have met in church as well as in the market place.

We do not hear much about interpreters – except in occasional official, legal or government transactions – so ordinary, everyday communication must have been tricky. Furthermore, society may not have been as residentially fixed in the seventeenth and eighteenth centuries as we sometimes believe: our forbears moved from parish to parish quite frequently. Even so, the linguistic mix after the Plantation must have resulted in people listening to pronunciations and words which they had never heard before, something we find difficult to imagine in an age when travel is so much easier and when we are all accustomed to radio, films and television.

For most people who lived in Ulster in the one hundred years after 1650, the conventions of writing down speech were not a problem although, as Philip Robinson has shown, in the early part of the seventeenth century written Scots differed very dramatically from written English.[3] I can vividly recall my sense of culture shock when I encountered, in the speech of Edinburgh, the last remnants of the old letter 'yogh' – which is spelled with a 'z' in modern writing, but not pronounced like modern z – in names like Dalzell and Menzies which are pronounced /di:yel/ and /mingis/. The anglicisation of written Scots, and the decline and virtual disappearance of its old letters and old spellings – like *quhen* for 'when' – can be documented in Scotland and, by extension, for Scots speakers in Ulster.

However, it is much more difficult to chart the relationship between eighteenth-century literary Scots – that is, the language as written by Burns in Scotland and by the poets of the Scots tradition in Ulster – and the standard written language used all over Britain from about 1700. By the mid-eighteenth century, the written form of Scots dialect is used chiefly to signal that the author is doing something unusual, that he is making some attempt to represent his speech phonetically. The standard spellings of English cannot represent the finer points of pronunciation but, in a sense, they do not have to. Similarly, spellings of Scots pronunciations and vocabulary have themselves become conventional, and had done so even by the time of the poets who wrote in Ulster, but may well not represent their actual speech forms. For instance, James Orr (1770-1816) uses the spelling *ance* for standard English 'once' but he may have used either 'wance' or 'yince' pronunciations.

All of this makes it difficult to interpret the written evidence, which is all we have. However, just now and then you suddenly get a beautiful insight which lets you understand how scholars *can* get their kicks from historical linguistics. For example, the weaver and poet Francis Boyle, who lived at Gransha, County Down, in the middle of the eighteenth century, talks about someone who lived at the 'Stay Brae'.[4] Fair enough: you make a mental note that Boyle was clearly familiar with the conventional Scots spelling of *brae*, meaning 'hill'. But something niggles at you, and you remember the Scots proverb, 'It takes a stout heart to a stigh brae', meaning a 'steep hill'; and you know that for modern Ulster-Scots speakers the verb 'to stay' is pronounced 'to stigh'; so Boyle's spelling clearly indicates that his pronunciation was 'stigh' as well.

Boyle was born, apparently, in the early eighteenth century, a little more than one hundred years after the official beginning of the Plantation of Ulster, when land grants by James VI and I provided up to 100,000 Scots and English with a whole range of new challenges. As we have seen, not the least of these were linguistic. By Boyle's time, the language situation had crystallized somewhat and we start to get contemporary descriptions of speech communities. These descriptions are doubly interesting: firstly, they provide irreplaceable evidence about what the observers observed; and, secondly, they provide evidence about the observers' own linguistic attitudes. A couple of short extracts may serve as illustration: they are what might be called synchronic descriptions but they are informed by a diachronic perspective.

The Rev. John Graham of Maghera, County Derry, wrote in 1814:

> In reporting the language and customs peculiar to this neighbourhood, attention must be paid to the usual division of the inhabitants into English, Irish and Scotch. The dialect and customs of these distinct races are as different from each other as their respective creeds. The members of the established church are denominated Englishmen, they speak with an accent less provincial than the Dissenters or Roman Catholics, the Scotch or Irish; and forming a kind of medium between these two discordant bodies of people in religious opinions, language and habits, are usually treated with respect and kindness by both. The Dissenters speak broad Scotch, and are in the habit of using terms and expressions long since obsolete, even in Scotland.[5]

At the same period, the Rev. Alexander Ross of Dungiven, County Derry, wrote:

> The other inhabitants of the parish betray, in their names, customs, etc. the characteristics of a Scottish origin; this is peculiarly observable in the six townlands of the manor of Freemore, where the broad Scotch dialect still prevails. To this general observation, however, the townland of Tiermeel forms a singular exception; there the original names of Broomfield, Williams, Posten, Philips, testify the remains of an English colony, which conjecture is fully confirmed by their manners, habits, religion and language, though this last is now somewhat antiquated, in a more particular manner among the old and respectable family of the Postens, we meet with terms and expressions which have long since ceased to be familiar, but to the readers of Spenser: with the exception indeed of the Scotch district above mentioned, the English spoken in this parish is remarkable for its correctness and purity.[6]

These descriptions, and others like them, demonstrate that, down to the nineteenth century, the national origins of some Ulster people were still identifiable in their speech. These marks of linguistic distinctiveness are highlighted by the writers against the increasingly pervasive standardization of speech which the clergy of the established Church and others of their class regarded as both norm and goal. Time and again in the eighteenth and nineteenth centuries, you find people writing about Scots speech as a 'disagreeable jargon', and urging the universal and speedy acceptance of 'an unerring fixed standard in our living language'.[7] I think, incidentally, that such people as clergymen were very strongly influenced against speech variation because of the concentration on the classical languages, especially Latin, in their training. In the form of Latin they would have been familiar with, there are no regional variations. It was only later in the nineteenth century that historical linguists teased out the changes in Latin which led to the development of the Romance languages.

However, let us return to attitudes towards Scots speech. I am unhappy about agreeing too closely with the views of those who had an 'invincible aversion to the Scotch language and the Scotch accent and the Irish',[8] but I must say I do feel that the development of an Ulster standard form of speech (just so long as it is an *Ulster* form of speech) is not a bad thing. In the Old Testament, in Judges 12, we read what happened to the unfortunate Ephraimites who said 'sibboleth' rather than 'shibboleth'. In the late twentieth century, it is bound to be less divisive if not even trained linguists can always distinguish Falls Road speakers from Shankill speakers.

The existence of a standard form alongside a regional variety also allows for subtleties of linguistic choice that increase the available vocabulary and allow social nuances to be represented in literature as well as in the context of social situations. The poets of the eighteenth century could, and frequently did, use both standard and Scots pronunciations of given words to facilitate rhyming: they could, for instance, rhyme between 'coughed' and 'soft' in one verse, and 'soft' and 'daft' in the next. Those who have access to both a standard and a regional form of speech are quite often, perhaps always, linguistically sophisticated and recognise the correlations between occasion, social class, and linguistic choice. In James Orr's poetry, for instance, we see evidence of this again and again. His long poem 'The Irish Cottier's Death and Burial' is a wonderful evocation of the events and feelings brought about by a death in a traditional Ulster-Scots community, where a shared sense of proper behaviour, of decorum and of the fitness of things is one of the strongest of social bonds. When the local minister comes in to visit the sick man, the rural inhabitants feel it to be appropriate to try 'to quat braid Scotch', even though the minister himself was most likely of Ulster-Scots background and had almost certainly attended university in either Glasgow or Edinburgh.[9]

The majority of the men who wrote poetry in the eighteenth century in Ulster spoke either English, strongly influenced by Scots or, perhaps more likely, an out-and-out dialect of the Scots language, in many respects similar to but not identical with the dialects of Scots found in west and central Scotland, for instance in Ayrshire and Renfrewshire. These poets were influenced in various ways by the existence of a higher-status dialect of English, as un-Scots as possible, which we can call 'standard Ulster' but which is, in turn, not identical to standard English. The poets were imbued with the entirely standard English conventions of representing this more formal variety of Ulster language in writing and, thanks to enhanced communications, increased literacy, and the developing book trade of their period, were also very strongly influenced by the poetry and prose produced in contemporary Britain. Theirs was perhaps the first generation to be so aware of the developments and fashions of the high literature of their own day.

Why then did they make the effort to write in Scots or, as one disgruntled pundit of the day put it to his friend Samuel Thomson of Templepatrick, 'Why so partial to the Scotch muse?'[10] I will look at this problem briefly under the second head of my discourse.

The nature of the Ulster-Scots language *community*

The Ulster poets of the eighteenth century have not received the critical attention that their work deserves. I will return to this assertion briefly in my final section, and Ivan Herbison will provide further discussion in the next paper; but at this point I want to concentrate on the linguistic reasons for the lack of attention paid to their work by non-Ulster critics. Ulster-Scots diction, unfamiliar spelling conventions and even the apparatus of glossaries, where they are provided, make the verse look uncouth to those who do not share the linguistic background and who are, for whatever reasons, not prepared to make the effort that scholars, hailing from Russia, Japan and Surrey, are willing to invest in the poetry of Robert Burns. The use of Ulster-Scots therefore, for good or ill, excludes some readers.

The poets' use of 'the language of [their] native glen' is clearly intended to involve, as strongly as possible, people from their own

background, for whom this form of speech evokes childhood memo-
ries, shared experiences and group solidarities.[11] It can be argued
that the use of Ulster-Scots is a way found by these poets – linguistically sophisticated as they are – of imaging their involvement with
their community. A shared language is one of the many strong bonds
holding their society together. In poem after poem, Orr, Thomson
and the others, rejoice in the mutual relationships:

> . . . where every trait of honest nature reigns
> Which links each heart in friendship's mystic chains.[12]

If time permitted, I would look at how the Ulster poets treated
Robert Burns as one of themselves, involving him in their community
by going to great lengths to visit him, to exchange presents with him,
and to hear news of his activities. A collection of letters addressed to
Samuel Thomson of Carngranny, near Templepatrick, holds many
examples of this interchange. In one letter, there is even a request
from Burns for a pound of Dublin snuff.[13] There are many examples
of Ulster poets using Burnsian diction and themes which, I would
argue, is their way of almost iconographically representing the bonds
between them. But, for the rest of this section, I shall concentrate on
James Orr of Ballycarry because the almost mystic perception of rootedness, of connectedness, is strongest in him. Orr's Masonic, millen-
nial and United Irish ideals, which undoubtedly affect his beliefs
about the nature of his community, must wait for another occasion:
for now I shall look at just one cluster of images and vocabulary which
will serve as pointers towards a fuller understanding of Orr's perception of the community in which he lived.

For Orr, one of the elements which characterise his society is the
kind of evaluation of individuals which is possible only in an inti-
mately structured community where everyone is known and where
everyone, as Orr remarks of his reading society associates, 'all my toils
and all my pastimes share'.[14] After the death of the cottier, in the
poem we looked at earlier:

> The village sires, wha kent him lang, lament
>   The dear deceas'd, an' praise his life an' creed;
>   For if they crav'd his help in time o' need,
> Or gied him trust, they prov'd him true an' kin'.[15]

Elsewhere he writes of the 'palm of posthumous applause', and of
how

> . . . these swains prepare the house of death,
> To hold the friend they lov'd and prais'd:[16]

The community has a right, perhaps even a duty, to assess the moral and social worth of its members, but probably only after their death.

The pathos of funeral rites performed for a shipwrecked stranger, someone unknown, whose family will never know his fate, strikes Orr very forcibly; and other poems suggest that 'a grave prepared by strangers' – to die unknown, far from the 'long loved shores' – is the saddest of all ends.[17] For Orr, and perhaps for others who have lived in Ulster, those who know who they are and who recognize those around them are characterised, must be characterised, by the behaviour and beliefs acknowledged by their community to be appropriate. Such a view of society can degenerate into an unthinking and narrow demand for rigid conformity, but for Orr, lucky perhaps not to have lived too long into the nineteenth century, it provided strength and self-awareness. His poems attempt to recreate the network of acquaintance, the shared experiences, and the communal judgements of a small area of east Antrim at one point in its history and, I believe, very largely succeed in so doing.

It is significant that this small area retained a knowledge of, and affection for, the work of one of its members for almost 200 years. Orr is still well known in Ballycarry today. I will finish this section by drawing your attention to some fascinating, thought-provoking but clearly unintentional parallels between the ideas Orr reveals in his verse and the physical presentation of his collected poems in a volume which was published in 1935 at the instigation of his local community, 170 years after his death.

The frontispiece is a picture of his cottage, with two lines which function almost like an epitaph on a gravestone:

> Here the toilsome loom he plied,
> Here he lived and wrote and – died.

The very existence of the 1935 volume belies Orr's fear that:

> . . . my foes ere long may blot
> My memory on thy ruin'd stead.[18]

(Here 'stead' stands for wallsteads or ruined remnants.) Included in the 1935 volume is a facsimile of the title page of the posthumous

Frontispiece, showing the cottage of James Orr (1770-1816), the Bard of Ballycarry, from the 1935 edition of his poems.

edition of 1817, with its quotation from Burns which firmly links Orr with both the Scottishness and the Freemasonry of the community of poets: 'Fareweel! my rhyme-composing brither'. The somewhat judgemental, though sympathetic, biography appended to the posthumous volume by Orr's friend Archy McDowell, is the precise equivalent of the community's posthumous assessment of one of its members:

> His name Broadisland shall revere,
> Nor fail to have him memoriz'd.[19]

a hope fulfilled by the 1935 volume.

The circumstances of the 1935 reprint have produced a further set of parallels, consideration of which will propel me into my third and final section. About twenty-five Ballycarry people were involved in republishing the poems of Orr in order, the preface says, that local men and women should remember him. Of their surnames, eleven are paralleled in the list of mainly south-Antrim subscribers gathered by Orr for his 1804 volume; both lists have a Miss McAllister – surely not the same woman! – and, in some cases, the surnames are linked with the same townlands.

The nature of the Ulster-Scots

In Orr's poems we hear the voice of someone who knows who he is. He speaks to his community in its own language. The people who bought his books were known, as most people in Ulster were until recently, by having the townland of their abode, or of their family's origin, appended to their surname: Orr of Ballycarry. One typical form of rural settlement here, the clachan, must have produced a certain kind of outlook on neighbours, farmwork sharing, and the nature of community: its sociology is perhaps unrecoverable. The local brand of Protestantism, Presbyterianism, is inherently parochial, in both senses of the word; its structures of government focus the minds of its adherents on local rather than world horizons. Genealogies reveal again and again – and I hope not just in my ancestry! – the inter-relatedness of families in a given area.

These are aspects of the Ulster-Scots community which could be explored, after more research. I am glad to note that more work is being done on Ulster's intellectual and social history but we have a lot to do to equal the output on, for instance, Edinburgh in the eighteenth century. The population of Ulster must have been greater

The tomb of the poet James Orr, in Ballycarry graveyard, erected by his fellow-Masons. From *The Ballycarry Bazaar*.

than that of Edinburgh in the period, and why, after all, should we accept the received wisdom that cities are intrinsically more important than rural areas?

I want to look now at an aspect of the relationship between Uster and Scotland which at first sight runs counter to the rootedness, the continuity, the importance of knowing who you are, which is so characteristic of James Orr. When I started thinking about Ulster and Scotland a few years ago, I was struck, as others, including the distin-

t, John Oliver, have been, by the apparent
affects Ulster Scots and Scottish Scots: nei-
retained much knowledge of the other.
ies who can say which parish in Scotland
stors, and it is still the more striking that
been totally forgotten in Scotland: there
friends in Ulster. Even in the nineteenth
itionary material could be gathered and,
thousands of people left Scotland only
e up with a quasi-pyschological hypothe-
o left Scotland felt in some sense guilty
notherland and blotted out the memo-
with the new environment.[21] This is an
ry, and perhaps a bit far-fetched. In
it the material for this paper, I came up
ins, to my satisfaction at least, not only
Scottish origins but also, perhaps, why
lectual history have not received ade-

the eighteenth century and, to some
, was enough. They did not need
radling institutions were in place, and
cally, socially and religiously compati-
ndividuals reached a certain critical
size. ...century poets, at their best, combined elements from a literary world outside the province with the familiar accents of their own community. This makes them fascinating still for Ulster readers today, but there is probably a subliminal message in their work, which is an automatic turnoff for literary critics whose intellectual allegiances – or, should I say, aspirations? – are metropolitan or even cosmopolitan. The Ulster-Scots poets, successfully imaging their involvement with a community which supplied all their emotional and intellectual needs, antagonise outsiders; in the twentieth century,

poets are supposed to be writing for at least a pan-Britannic readership and there is no critical allowance made for those who write, first and foremost, for a regional audience. A similar subliminal message may still be flashing in the perceptions of those in London and Dublin and Washington who believe that they are trying to understand the Ulster psyche; it seems to me that at least some of Ulster's image problem derives from the aggrievement of those who dimly understand that, at some level, Ulster is still 'enough' for those who live here.

All things change, even the Ulster-Scots community, and in the late twentieth century not many can be as sure of where they belong as were Orr of Ballycarry and Thomson of Carngranny, or even the more numerous, mute, inglorious Browns of Ballinaloob, Wallaces of Broghanor and Pinkertons of Secon. We certainly can, and perhaps should, re-examine and learn more about the 'enoughness' of Ulster. Yet we might also look at other ways of belonging which did not much interest the earlier Ulster-Scots but which might prove to be more inclusive. Origins in Scotland, yes certainly, and perhaps in this conference we can pool our ideas on ways to reach back beyond the amnesia, but also English and Irish origins, and links between Ulster and other places on the Atlantic seaboard. It seems that Ulster is still perceived as being doomed to oscillate mutely between the rival attractions of Dublin and London but in truth neither city has much to say to, or much understanding of, the mentality of life in the provinces of a provincial city. Ulster folk have something to contribute to, and more to learn from, discussions with Glasgow, or Galway, or Grenoble, or Greenville, North Carolina, and their surrounding regions, than from any metropolitan culture.

And here, after the only bit of thunder I have permitted myself, is the long withheld text of this discourse. I have taken it from J.B. Killen's fascinating purple prose address 'The Spirit of Irish History', read, very appropriately, before the Literary and Scientific Society of Queen's College, Belfast, at the closing meeting of its twentieth session in 1870:

> Ignorance of the past will not save us from the bitterness of the present. Let there be light, that we may see each other, and whence we came.[22]

NOTES

1. Brendan Adams, 'Common [consonantal] features in Ulster Irish and Ulster English' in Michael Barry and Philip Tilling (eds), *The English Dialects of Ulster: an Anthology of Articles on Ulster Speech by G.B. Adams* (Holywood: Ulster

Folk and Transport Museum, 1986) pp. 105-112.

2. Brendan Adams, 'Aspects of monoglottism in Ulster', in Barry and Tilling (eds), *The English Dialects of Ulster*, p. 119.

3. Philip Robinson, 'The Scots Language in seventeenth-century Ulster', *Ulster Folklife*, vol. 35, 1989, pp. 86-99.

4. Francis Boyle, *Miscellaneous Poems* (Belfast, 1811) p. 8.

5. William S. Mason, *A Statistical Account or Parochial Survey of Ireland*, Vol. 1 (Dublin: pr. Graisberry and Campbell, 1814) p. 592.

6. ibid, p. 320.

7. ibid, p. 259; *Belfast Mercury*, 19 March 1784.

8. 'Civilis', *Belfast News Letter*, 8 June 1792.

9. James Orr, 'The Irish Cottier's Death and Burial', in *Poems on Various Subjects by James Orr of Ballycarry, with a Sketch of his Life* [1804, 1817] (Belfast: Mullan, 1935) p. 261.

10. Letter from W.H. Drummond to Samuel Thomson, 29 December 1798, MS 7257, Trinity College, Dublin. The author is grateful to the Board of Trinity College, Dublin, for permission to quote from this manuscript.

11. Thomas Beggs, *The Second Part of the Minstrel's Offering* (Belfast, 1836) preface.

12. John McKinley, *The Giant's Causeway: A Poem; with, The Traveller Benighted in Mourne*. 2nd ed. (Dublin, 1821) p. 43.

13. T. House[?], letter to Samuel Thomson, 3 March 1791, MS 7257, Trinity College, Dublin. The author is grateful to the Board of Trinity College, Dublin, for permission to quote from this manuscript.

14. James Orr, 'The Reading Society', *Poems on Various Subjects*, p. 274.

15. James Orr, 'The Irish Cottier's Death and Burial', *Poems on Various Subjects*, p. 265.

16. James Orr, 'Elegy Written in the Churchyard of Templecorran', *Poems on Various Subjects*, p. 130; 'Lines on Seeing the First Grave Made in a New Graveyard', *Poems on Various Subjects*, p. 253.

17. James Orr, 'Elegy Composed at the Interment of a Shipwrecked Stranger', *Poems on Various Subjects*, p. 245; 'The Banks of Larne', *Poems on Various Subjects*, p. 69.

18. James Orr, 'The Banks of Larne', *Poems on Various Subjects*, p. 68.

19. A. McDowell, 'Elegiac Stanzas on the Death of the Author', in James Orr, *Poems on Various Subjects*, p. 194.

20. John A. Oliver, 'Some Ulster Scots and their origin in Scotland', *Familia*, vol. 2, no. 3, 1987, p. 104.

21. Linde Lunney, 'Ulster attitudes to Scottishness: the eighteenth century and after' in Ian S. Wood (ed.) *Scotland and Ulster* (Edinburgh: Mercat Press, 1994), p. 58.

22. J.B. Killen, *The Spirit of Irish History. A Paper read before the Literary and Scientific Society of Queen's College, Belfast, at the Closing Meeting of its Twentieth Session* (Dublin, 1870).

Postscript: I am happy to record a modern instance of the memorializing of James Orr: the Cultural Traditions Group, organisers of the 'Varieties of Scottishness' Conference in March 1996, have through the Local Traditions Grants Scheme helped Ballycarry Community Association to map Ballycarry graveyard where James Orr is buried, and have, in so doing, reinforced both his memory and contemporary community awareness of history: *Giving Voices: the Work of the Cultural Traditions Group, 1990-1994* (Belfast: CTG, 1995) p. 16.

'THE REST IS SILENCE':
SOME REMARKS ON THE DISAPPEARANCE OF
ULSTER-SCOTS POETRY

Ivan Herbison

John Dunlop has recently remarked that many members of the Presbyterian community today 'feel like an invisible people. It is as if they do not exist.'[1] Today I wish to examine some aspects of the work of some 'invisible' poets, and explore the disappearance of their distinctive literary and cultural tradition which took its inspiration from Scotland. At the first Cultural Traditions Group Conference, 'Varieties of Irishness' (1989), Michael Longley identified a prevalent tendency 'to undervalue, even to ignore, the Scottish horizon'.[2] However, in the subsequent conferences, 'Varieties of Britishness' (1990) and 'All Europeans Now?' (1991), this 'Scottish horizon' all but vanished. Therefore I welcome this belated opportunity to focus attention on aspects of Scottish cultural influence in Ulster. All too often Ulster-Scots language, literature, and culture have been excluded, ignored, sidelined, or treated as a mere afterthought. The continued neglect of Ulster-Scots is in no small measure due to the prevailing orthodoxy in cultural and political circles of the idea of 'two traditions'. This binary framework not merely distorts the complex realities of cultural diversity; it renders invisible a 'third tradition', that of 'the Scottish horizon'.

Nowhere is the influence of Scottish linguistic, literary, and cultural traditions more clearly evident than in the work of the Rhyming Weavers.[3] These working-class poets wrote in both English and in Ulster-Scots but it is their vernacular poems which constitute their distinctive contribution to the cultural history of Ireland. The weaver poets are closely associated with the main areas of Scottish settlement. Although there is evidence of a thriving tradition of 'Scotch poems' from the Laggan district of east Donegal,[4] the majority of the poets were concentrated in County Antrim and County Down. South-east Antrim was the focus of an important group comprising James

Campbell of Ballynure (1758-1818), Samuel Thomson of Carngranny (1766-1816), James Orr of Ballycarry (1770-1816), and Thomas Beggs of Ballyclare (1789-1847). Beggs, born at Glenwherry, was a close friend of the leading figure of the mid-Antrim group, David Herbison of Dunclug (1800-1880). The most prominent poets from Down were Andrew McKenzie of Dunover (1780-1839), Hugh Porter of Moneyslane (born 1781), and Robert Huddleston of Moneyrea (1814-1887). Yet a tradition which had been flourishing in the early 1800s had all but disappeared by the end of the nineteenth century. In this present century these poets are largely forgotten figures, and their works now attract little critical attention. In this paper I wish to examine three aspects of the disappearance of Ulster-Scots poetry. Firstly, I will consider the reasons for the decline of the Rhyming Weavers in the nineteenth century. Secondly, I will explore the significance of the adoption and abandonment of the vernacular as a literary medium. Finally, I will examine aspects of the critical reception of Ulster-Scots poetry and its disappearance from the canon of Irish writing.

The decline of the Rhyming Weavers

Just as the origins of the Rhyming Weavers owed much to the prosperity made possible by the growth of the linen industry, so their decline was a consequence of changing economic and social conditions. As working-class poets, writing for a working-class audience, they were peculiarly vulnerable to fluctuations in the economic climate. The transformation of weaving from a rural craft into an urban, factory-based industrial process destroyed the prosperity of the hand-loom weavers. Between 1800 and 1840 a weaver's weekly wages were reduced from £1 18s 0d to 6s 3d.[5] This had a devastating impact on the rural communities in Antrim and Down which were sustained by the combination of farming and weaving. As Dr Linde Lunney has pointed out, the Ulster-Scots cultural identity is very much based on a sense of belonging to stable rural communities. Unlike James Orr, who apart from one brief period spent all his life in Ballycarry, the poets of the later nineteenth century faced the disruptions of industrialisation, urbanisation, and emigration.[6] Thomas Beggs left the bleach greens of Ballyclare and came to Belfast to seek employment in a chemical bleach factory.[7] There were many poets amongst the great exodus of emigrants from Ireland during the nineteenth century. James McHenry of Larne (1785-1845), John Smyth of Ballymena (1783-1854), and Henry McD. Flecher of Moneyrea (1827-c.1909) all left for

America.[8] David Herbison of Dunclug emigrated to Quebec in 1827 but was shipwrecked and returned home to Ballymena. Yet his three brothers and all but one of his children joined the exodus. Of the later poets, only David Herbison succeeded in retaining both his connection with the linen trade and his links to a local community.[9]

Another factor in the decline of the Rhyming Weavers was the introduction of a new education policy in the 1830s, which further marginalised Scottish cultural influence. Up until the early nineteenth century educational provision was private rather than public, and many of the weaver poets were self-educated.[10] State control of education through the National School system enabled the Anglo-Irish establishment to frame a curriculum which was designed to emphasise English language, literature, and cultural values, which regarded Ulster-Scots as a debased dialect, and which failed to reflect Ulster's Scottish cultural heritage.

The nineteenth century was also a period of considerable religious upheaval for Presbyterians.[11] In the first half of the century there was the conflict between Orthodoxy and Remonstrance, between Henry Cooke and Henry Montgomery, which led to the separation of the Remonstrants in 1829 and to the union of the Synod of Ulster and the Secession Synod in 1840. In the second half of the century there occurred the 1859 Revival which changed the nature of Presbyterian culture. The evangelical fervour which it aroused did much to revive puritan objections to literature and the arts. The impact of the Revival on Presbyterian culture has yet to be fully assessed, but Norman Vance makes a valuable point in drawing attention to the opposition between literature and belief:

> When the Revival was at its height an Armagh bookseller reported that he had not sold a single novel for three weeks, implying a perceived incompatibility between novel-reading and born-again religious seriousness.[12]

The decline of the Rhyming Weavers may well owe something to the rejection by mainstream Presbyterianism of 'New Licht' liberalism, and to the strengthening of puritan scruples about the arts which the Revival encouraged.

An additional factor in the decline of the Rhyming Weavers was their alienation from the changing political aspirations of the majority of Presbyterians. Under the leadership of Cooke, the Presbyterian community aligned itself with conservatism and unionism. However,

many of the Rhyming Weavers retained an attachment to the radical
Dissenting tradition and the ideals of 1798. The nineteenth century
saw, on the one hand, the birth of the United Kingdom (1801) and
the development of the ideology of imperialism and, on the other,
the increasing identification of Irish nationalism with Gaelic culture
and Catholicism.[13] Caught between these two forces, the Rhyming
Weavers were marginalised. It is not surprising that some of the poets
sensed the tension between their political and cultural allegiances:

> I love my native land, no doubt,
>   Attach'd to her thro' thick and thin,
> Yet tho' I'm *Irish* all *without,*
>   I'm every item *Scotch within.*[14]

To be taken seriously by the literary establishment, the Rhyming
Weavers also had to write in English, and the problems in addressing
these two audiences were not lost on James Orr:

> Nor fame, nor fortune, I from verse expect,
> Alike undone by beauty and defect,
> My rude Scotch rhymes the tasteful justly slight,
> The Scotch-tongued rustics scorn each nobler flight.[15]

If Orr represents Ulster-Scots culture at the height of its self-
confidence, Herbison is the poet who records its decline. His work
records the hardship which resulted from the introduction of the
steam loom:

> For ah! I'm sure I'll never see
> Such joys as charmed my youthfu' e'e –
> The days are past when folks like me
>   Could earn their bread,
> My auld wheel now sits silently
>   Aboon the bed.

> And well may Erin weep and wail
> The day the wheels began to fail;
> Our tradesmen now can scarce get kail
>   Betimes to eat,
> In shipfuls they are doomed to sail
>   In quest o' meat!

For that machine that spins the yarn
Left us unfit our bread to earn;
O Erin! will you ne'er turn stern
   Against your foe,
When every auld wife can discern
   Your overthrow.[16]

The famine of 1846-1848 roused his indignation and sharpened his
social and political conscience:

To pay the laird his rent
   Our claes were a' to pawn –
Nane to heed my sad lament –
   No a frien' to take my han'!

I'm now without a hame
   For my little bairns and me;
And to beg I think a shame,
   Where a beggar needna be.

But Erin's held in scorn,
   Peace she canna find ava –
Neglected and forlorn
   Are her children ane and a'.

To the workhouse I maun go,
   In its hated wa's to dee,
Where the bitter sound of woe
   Never yet has ceased to be.[17]

Herbison's sympathy for the radical Dissenting tradition more
often took a lyrical rather than a political form. He continued to write
about the 1798 Rebellion in terms of its impact on individuals. His
poems of exile seek to portray a sense of loss and alienation. Even in
1877 Herbison was still writing about the events of 1798:

I now am left an exile here
Of friends bereft who loved me dear;
Nor have I hope that e'er I'll see
Their smile bring life's joys back to me . . .

THE

SELECT WORKS

OF

DAVID HERBISON.

WITH

LIFE OF THE AUTHOR,

BY REV. DAVID M'MEEKIN,

BALLYMENA.

BELFAST:—WILLIAM MULLAN & SON.

BALLYMENA:—JOHN WIER AND MOSES ERWIN.

LONDONDERRY:—JOHN HEMPTON.

The title page of the porthumous edition of Herbison's works (1883). His community celebrated Herbison with this edition and a memorial in the graveyard in Ballymena, a memorial unique among the weaver poets.

> But ah! I fear my wish is vain,
> I still must bear the Exile's chain;
> And only in my dreams I'll see
> Her beauty where I'll never be . . .
>
> But ah! we failed to break the chain
> Which long has held our Isle in pain . . .
> My latest prayer in life shall be
> That Erin ne'er may discord see.[18]

But during his long life his radical sympathies have been transmuted from a political consciousness to an emotional attachment. Separated from the mainstream of Ulster-Scots politics, he identifies with the figure of the exile in his ballads.

Herbison's work best illustrates the final cause in the decline of the Rhyming Weavers. In order to continue publishing his work in newspapers and popular local periodicals, he was increasingly forced to write in standard English rather than in Ulster-Scots. Even his friend and fellow-poet, John Fullarton, is contemptuous of Herbison's 'Scotch rhymes'.[19] The gradual abandonment of Ulster-Scots deprived him of his most distinctive voice and impoverished his work. Robert Huddleston of Moneyrea also suffered from this prejudice against the vernacular. He had published two volumes of poetry in the 1840s[20] but was unable to publish any more, although he continued to write in a highly individual Ulster-Scots until his death in 1887, protesting to the end against cultural and linguistic marginalisation.[21] The rest is silence.

Ulster-Scots as a literary medium

Consideration of the difficulties of publishing literary work in Ulster-Scots towards the end of the nineteenth century brings me to my second theme: the decline in the status of the vernacular and its abandonment as a literary medium. It is useful to review briefly the status of the vernacular in Scotland before turning to the situation in Ulster.

Scots (or 'Inglis' as it is often called in the Middle Ages) descends from the Northumbrian dialect of Old English but, unlike other regional dialects of English, it became the language of an independent nation and produced a flourishing literature, including the poets Dunbar and Henryson. It was distinctive not merely in pronunciation but also in vocabulary, syntax, and orthography. The succession of James VI to the throne of England marked the end of Scots as an independent language and it began to give way to English. The revival of vernacular Scots in the eighteenth century can be seen as a cultural response to the Act of Union (1707) which removed the last vestige of political independence. The use of the vernacular was thus a cultural expression of nationalism. It is no surprise that many of the leading figures of the revival, from Allan Ramsay (1686-1758) to James Hogg, the Ettrick Shepherd (1770-1835), had Jacobite sympathies.[22] Although Robert Burns (1759-1796) never fully identified with the Jacobite cause, songs such as 'Scots, wha hae wi' Wallace bled' combine the evocation of a traditional Scottish national hero with the ideals of liberty and freedom espoused by the French Revolution.[23]

Ulster-Scots poets and readers were acutely conscious of their Scottish cultural heritage. Scottish vernacular poems were printed in Belfast as early as 1700; and the works of Ramsay and Burns were printed many times between 1740 and 1800.[24] David Herbison made two separate journeys from Ballymena to Belfast to obtain copies of Ramsay and Burns, and declared that his favourite poet was James Hogg.[25] The importance of Burns for the Rhyming Weavers lay in his creation of a regional literature, strongly vernacular in idiom and nationalist in tone and sentiment. They sought to forge their own regional/national linguistic identity.

Language is inherently political. For the Rhyming Weavers, Ulster-Scots was a means of asserting their independence of English. It makes both a political and a cultural statement. None of the Ulster poets was Jacobite, but they sympathised with the egalitarian aims of the French and American Revolutions. Conversely, suspicion of the Ulster-Scots and prejudice against their ain native tung reveal an underlying anxiety about their ultimate loyalties. The hostility towards both language and people is widespread. It is voiced by William Carleton and by the writers of the Ordnance Survey Memoirs in the 1830s:

> In the language and expressions of the northern peasantry he [the author] has studiously avoided that intolerable Scoto-Hibernic jargon which pierces the ear so unmercifully, but he has preserved everything Irish . . . so that the book, wherever it may go, will exhibit a truly Hibernian spirit.[26]

Their accent is peculiarly and among the old people disagreeably strong and broad. Their idioms and saws are strictly Scottish, and many of them are pithy and quaint.[27]

Their disagreeable Scottish manner would to a stranger stamp them as rude and uncourteous.[28]

The decline of the vernacular coincided with the growth of unionist and imperialist ideologies which placed London at the centre and downgraded Ulster-Scots. Instead of being a source of cultural pride and solidarity it became a hindrance to economic and social betterment, a sign of backwardness to be emended and corrected. Standard English was the medium for progress and self-improvement.[29]

This situation is vividly illustrated in Herbison's poem 'My Ain Native Toun'. The original title was 'An Auld Body's Notions o' the Improvements in Ballymena'. The narrator chronicles the changes which have turned skilled craftsmen into exploited factory workers:

Until we ceased selling our claith in the hall,
Nae want was amang us our peace to enthrall,
For a' kind o' work we had plenty o' cash,
And merchants that ne'er cut a bit o' a dash;
They were perfectly honest, kind, friendly, and true,
And knew weel the wark they cam' weekly to do;
The house-money never went into their fabs,
It went to the house that took care o' our wabs!
And wad it still go for the use it did then,
The weaver wad pay't like a dash o' his pen;
But oh, what a change on a' things has cam' roun'
Since I was a boy in my ain native toun . . .

Oh had I the power the past to restore,
The reel wad still crack and the spinning wheel snore,
Mill-yarn wad sink doun as it never had been,
Trade flourish as fair as it ever was seen;
Distress and oppression flee far frae our view,
Our hamlets rejoice and their beauties renew;
The profligate band that brought want to our door
Should labour or starve on a far foreign shore;
A wab in a steamloom should never appear,
Our country to steep in affliction and fear;
Peace, pleasure, and plenty, and happy hearts roun'
And times wad revive in my ain native toun.[30]

The vernacular Ulster-Scots which the narrator uses is itself a powerful symbol of what has passed away, like the hand-looms and the spinning wheels. All he can do is to cling on to the vain hope that 'times
wad revive in my ain native toun'.

   The death of David Herbison brought to a close the age of the
Rhyming Weavers but it did not entirely mark the end of Ulster-Scots
poetry. Thomas Given and Adam Lynn of Cullybackey continued the
tradition into the early years of this century.[31] Later still W.F. Marshall
published his *Ballads and Verses from Tyrone* (1929) and *Ballads from
Tyrone* (1939). The latter included his celebrated 'Me an' Me Da':

> I'm livin' in Drumlister,
> An' I'm gettin very oul',
> I have to wear an Indian bag
> To save me from the coul'.
> The deil a man in this townlan'
> Wos claner raired nor me,
> But I'm livin' in Drumlister
> In clabber to the knee.[32]

But Marshall's work is not merely retrospective and nostalgic; it is
regressive. Acute social comment has been replaced by the comic
caricature, sympathy by ironic distance. Marshall was the last poet to
make serious literary use of Ulster-Scots but the tradition had
nowhere to go but backwards. The rest is silence.

Ulster-Scots poetry and Anglo-Irish literature

Because of their complex literary and linguistic background the
Rhyming Weavers inevitably occupy an anomalous position in Irish
literary history and pose problems of definition. Their very existence
challenges the concept of 'Anglo-Irish' literature. Could they be considered to belong instead to the Scottish literary tradition from which
they drew their inspiration? Then what are we to make of their
English verse, and their sense of Irishness? However, contemporary
reviewers of the weaver poets sensed no such complexities. A collection of reviews of David Herbison's published volumes provides an
insight into the critical reception of his works by the literary establishment of his day.

   These reviews reveal two prevalent attitudes. Herbison is perceived
as a self-taught 'child of nature', the embodiment of spontaneous

romantic Genius, both a natural poet and a poet of nature. As such, he is treated with both literary and social condescension:

> David is a weaver, and speaks directly to his own class. Indirectly, he addresses himself to such of the upper classes as do not demand extraordinary niceties . . . He sings, like the bird on the bush, to please himself.

> His opportunities have been few, but he has made the best use of them . . . The child of simplicity – the poet of rural life – his offering is but a wreath of wild flowers.

> It is refreshing, after a weary study of the spasmodic poets of our day . . . to turn to the modest lay of David Herbison, which, whatever its faults, judged by high poetic standards, manifests a deep love of Nature.

On the other hand, his poems in 'the Antrim Doric', are regarded as imitations of Burns:

> A few of them are confessed imitations of Burns, in sentiment, dialect, and rhythm, and are valuable as a pleasing reflex of the manners of the country people in Mr. Herbison's neighbourhood.

> His style is simple and unaffected, more in the manner of Burns than of any other modern poet; and with a verse now and then that is very Burnslike in expression and treatment.

> The Scottish Doric, in which Burns spoke . . . has furnished Mr Herbison with, in many of his poems, a medium in which to express . . . the tender emotions of the human heart.[33]

This misapprehension of their relationship to Burns preoccupied the Ulster-Scots poets. Thomas Beggs feels the need to justify his use of dialect:

> Should the reader of the following effusions suppose, that in some parts the Author has imitated the Scottish Dialect, he would wish to correct the idea by alleging that he has written in his own style – in the language of his native glen – not constrained but spontaneous as the lispings of our first speech.[34]

Robert Huddleston protests passionately against the same false impu-
tation:

> What a mockery it is then, for intelligent men to be calling the writ-
> ings of some authors those of others, because they resemble them
> in language. Thus it is that so many rustic authors of Ulster are said
> to be sprung from Burns.[35]

The accusation that the Rhyming Weavers are imitators of Burns, who
merely copy his language, verse forms and subject matter, was taken
up by literary historians, biographers and bibliographers such as
O'Donoghue and Crone,[36] and is still encountered today, despite
Hewitt's efforts to vindicate them.[37]

If the Rhyming Weavers resemble Burns, it is because they are heirs
to the same literary and linguistic traditions:

> The Ulster rural tradition stemmed from the Scots, developed on
> parallel lines, so that it was able to receive nurture from the Burns
> source, but at the same time, bear a foliage in some degree
> modified by the Irish climate.[38]

What they did seek to imitate was his achievement in establishing a distinctive regional literature. The accusation that they were imitators of
Burns all too conveniently removes the Ulster poets from consideration as genuine literary figures, and denies them cultural integrity.

The Rhyming Weavers maintained a token presence in Irish literary history until the early years of the present century through their
inclusion in several anthologies in the belles-lettrist tradition.[39] Since
then they have disappeared both from literary history and from the
canon of Irish writers. Anglo-Irish literature would appear to have
little room for poets who deliberately adopted a Scottish cultural
model. Seamus Deane's *Short History of Irish Literature* proves the
point.[40] Not only is there no mention of the Ulster-Scots poets but the
whole construction of Irish literary history presented by Deane
denies the very existence of these literary dissenters. Deane is quite
explicit about the criteria for inclusion in 'the central story' of Irish
literature:

> That story is about a literary tradition which has undergone a series
> of revivals and collapses, all of them centred upon the idea of
> Ireland.[41]

But Deane's view of Ireland and Irish literature is irredeemably monist, predicated upon an assumption of a national and cultural unity which excludes the Ulster-Scots. After all, that is the shortest way with dissenters. Deane's approach is sadly typical. The only recent work of literary history to make significant mention of a Rhyming Weaver is Norman Vance's *Irish Literature: A Social History*.[42]

The cultural marginalisation of Ulster-Scots by the *Field Day Anthology of Irish Writing*,[43] edited by Deane, is merely the most recent and most blatant example of a more widespread reluctance to acknowledge the presence of a Scottish cultural heritage in Ulster. In the compass of three ample volumes, containing over 4,000 pages, there is, apparently, no room for a single poem in the vernacular Ulster-Scots. The *Anthology* announces its intention:

> to provide a commanding view of the various traditions of writing from AD550 to the late twentieth century – in Irish, English, Latin, and Norman-French – that have helped to nurture one of the most distinctive literatures in the world.[44]

There is not even a mention of Scottish influence.

Of course, the *Field Day Anthology* is more than a mere exercise in picking and choosing texts. It is an attempt to define and construct a version of Irishness. Its political agenda is clearly nationalist. The view of Irish writing presented in the anthology is that of a dialectic between an autochthonous native tradition and a foreign colonialist tradition, and owes much to post-colonial theory.[45] Given this framework, it is hardly surprising that Ulster-Scots finds itself sidelined from the debate and conveniently ignored. As so often in the past, Field Day has chosen to define Irishness by exclusion.

The reaction to Field Day's treatment of Ulster-Scots has been predictably muted. When Damian Smyth, in his review of the *Anthology* accused it of committing an act of 'intellectual ethnic cleansing',[46] the editorial of the *Linen Hall Review* took pains to justify the exclusion of the Rhyming Weavers by rehearsing the old arguments about imitation of Burns, thus condoning with apparent equanimity Field Day's act of cultural censorship.[47] The *Anthology*'s exclusion of Ulster-Scots is both studied and deliberate, for two English poems by James Orr are included in a section entitled 'Anglo-Irish Verse 1675-1825'.[48] This is a somewhat Procrustean bed for the Bard of Ballycarry: the Orr of 'The Irishman' is acceptable, while the Orr of 'Donegore Hill' and 'The Irish Cottier's Death and Burial' is consigned to cultural oblivion. The rest is silence.

A future for Ulster-Scots?

A consequence of Field Day and the debate which it engendered has been to strengthen the conviction of some of those concerned about Ulster-Scots that they must begin to set their own cultural agenda. The foundation of the Ulster-Scots Language Society and an Ulster-Scots Academy, and the establishment of *Ullans*, the Society's journal, bear witness to a renewed desire to promote knowledge and appreciation of Ulster-Scots language and literature. A new dialect dictionary has appeared[49] and James Fenton has recently published a valuable record of the living language.[50]

The declared aim of the Society is 'to promote the status of Ulster-Scots as a language and to re-establish its dignity'. This task will require discrimination and sensitivity. While few would quarrel with these aims, there are risks inherent in this approach. There is a real danger of creating an Ulster-Scots cultural ghetto through excessive introspection and a sense of cultural separation and self-sufficiency. Retreating into 'a place apart' is an understandable response to a widespread sense of exclusion. It is, moreover, a reaction typical of a culture resonant with Old Testament typology and New Testament doctrines of separation. Yet this response merely underlines and confirms exclusion.

In its promotion of Ulster-Scots language and literature *Ullans* will have to consider what audience it is seeking to address, its 'ain folk' or a wider cultural community. There is an urgent need to speak to that wider audience. It is time to challenge attempts, such as that of Field Day, to marginalise Ulster-Scots culture, to deprive it of its ain native tung, and to suppress its legitimate claim to be heard in the debate on cultural traditions. I hope that *Ullans* will follow the example of the Rhyming Weavers and address both audiences. But this debate belongs to the future and to another day.

NOTES

1. John Dunlop, *A Precarious Belonging: Presbyterians and the Conflict in Ireland* (Belfast: Blackstaff Press, 1995) p. 3.
2. Michael Longley, 'Address' in Maurna Crozier (ed.), *Cultural Traditions in Northern Ireland: 'Varieties of Irishness': Proceedings of the Cultural Traditions Group Conference, 3-4 March 1989* (Belfast: Institute of Irish Studies, 1989) p. 34.

3. See, John Hewitt, *Rhyming Weavers and other Country Poets of Antrim and Down* (Belfast: Blackstaff Press, 1974).
4. See, Ronnie Adams, '"Scotch Poems" from east Donegal in 1753', *Ullans*, no. 1, Spring 1993, pp. 24-25.
5. John Hewitt, 'Ulster poets, 1800-1870', unpublished MA thesis, the Queen's University of Belfast, 1951, p. 113.
6. For a fuller treatment of displacement and its cultural impact, see, Ivan Herbison, 'A sense of place: landscape and locality in the work of the Rhyming Weavers' in Gerald Dawe and John Wilson Foster (eds), *The Poet's Place: Ulster Literature and Society: Essays in Honour of John Hewitt, 1907-87* (Belfast: Institute of Irish Studies, 1991) pp. 63-75.
7. John Fullarton, 'Life of Thomas Beggs' in *The Poetical Works of Thomas Beggs* (Ballyclare: S. Corry, [1867]) p. vi.
8. On James McHenry and Henry McD. Flecher, see, D.J. O'Donoghue, *The Poets of Ireland: a Biographical and Bibliographical Dictionary of Irish Writers of English Verse* (Dublin: Hodges, Figgis, 1912); on John Smyth, see, David Herbison, 'John Smith – "Magowan"', *Ulster Magazine*, vol. 2, no. 23, November 1861, pp. 441-444.
9. See, *The Select Works of David Herbison. With Life of the author, by Rev. David McMeekin, Ballymena* (Belfast: Mullan; Ballymena: Wier and Erwin, [1883]), hereafter *Select Works*. For fuller accounts of David Herbison, see the introduction to my edition of a selection of his poems, *Webs of Fancy: Poems of David Herbison, the Bard of Dunclug* (Ballymena: Dunclug Press, 1980) and my article 'David Herbison, the Bard of Dunclug: a poet and his community, 1800-1880' in Eull Dunlop (ed.), *Mid Antrim 1983: Articles on the History of Ballymena and District* (Ballymena: Mid-Antrim Historical Group, 1983) pp. 102-130, also published separately (Ballymena: Dunclug Press, 1988).
10. See Linde Lunney, 'Knowledge and Enlightenment: attitudes to education in early nineteenth-century east Ulster', in Mary Daly and David Dickson (eds), *The Origins of Popular Literacy in Ireland: Language Change and Educational Development, 1700-1920* (Dublin: Department of Modern History, TCD, and Department of Modern History, UCD, 1990) pp. 97-111.
11. For a convenient treatment of Presbyterianism during the period, see, R. F. G. Holmes, *Our Irish Presbyterian Heritage* (Belfast: Publications Committee of the Presbyterian Church in Ireland, 1985) chaps 3-4, pp. 55-141.
12. Norman Vance, 'Presbyterian culture and Revival', *Bulletin of the Presbyterian Historical Society of Ireland*, vol. 22 , 1993, pp. 16-19 (p. 17).
13. See David Hempton, *Religion and Political Culture in Britain and Ireland: from the Glorious Revolution to the Decline of Empire* (Cambridge: Cambridge University Press, 1996) chap. 4, 'The making of the Irish Catholic nation', pp. 72-92.
14. Samuel Thomson, 'To Captain M'Dougall, Castle-Upton: with a Copy of the Author's Poems' in Ernest McA. Scott and Philip Robinson (eds), *The Country Rhymes of Samuel Thomson, the Bard of Carngranny, 1766-1816* (Bangor: Pretani Press, 1992) p. 62 (The Folk Poets of Ulster series, vol. 3).
15. James Orr, 'Address to Noah Dalway, of Bella-Hill, Esq.', *Poems on Various Subjects* (Belfast: Mullan, 1935) p. 235.
16. David Herbison, 'The Auld Wife's Lament for her Teapot', *Select Works*, p. 45.
17. David Herbison, 'The Irish Widow's Lament', *Select Works*, p. 49.
18. David Herbison, 'The Ulster Exile 1798', *Select Works*, pp. 292-293.

19. John Fullarton, 'Sketches of Ulster poets: David Herbison, the Bard of Dunclug', *Ulster Magazine*, vol. 2., no. 23 , November 1861, pp. 457-464 (p. 460).

20. Robert Huddleston, *A Collection of Poems and Songs on Rural Subjects* (Belfast: Smyth, 1844); *A Collection of Poems and Songs on Different Subjects* (Belfast: privately printed, 1846).

21. J.R.R. Adams, 'A rural bard, his printers and his public: Robert Huddleston of Moneyrea', *Linen Hall Review*, vol. 9, no. 3/4, Winter 1992, pp. 9-11.

22. See, Murray G. H. Pittock, *Poetry and Jacobite Politics in Eighteenth-Century Britain and Ireland* (Cambridge: Cambridge University Press, 1994) pp. 133-186.

23. ibid, pp. 215-222.

24. See, J.R.R. Adams, *The Printed Word and the Common Man: Popular Culture in Ulster, 1700-1900* (Belfast: Institute of Irish Studies, 1987) Appendix I: 'Ulster publications, 1699-1800', pp. 175-181.

25. Fullarton, 'Sketches of Ulster poets: David Herbison', p. 458.

26. [William Carleton], *Traits and Stories of the Irish Peasantry*, 2 vols (Dublin: Currie, 1830) preface.

27. 'Parish of Carnmoney, County Antrim' in Angélique Day and Patrick McWilliams (eds), *Ordnance Survey Memoirs of Ireland. Volume Two: Parishes of County Antrim*, I (Belfast: Institute of Irish Studies, 1990) p. 63.

28. Eull Dunlop and Ivan Herbison (eds), *Ordnance Survey Memoir (1830-38) for The Grange of Shilvodan, County Antrim* (Ballymena: Braid Books and Dunclug Press, 1990) p. 20.

29. See, for example, David Patterson, *The Provincialisms of Belfast and the Surrounding Districts Pointed out and Corrected* (Belfast: Mayne, 1860).

30. David Herbison, 'My Ain Native Toun', *Select Works*, pp. 306-307.

31. Thomas Given, *Poems from College and Country, by Three Brothers* (Belfast: Baird, 1900); Adam Lynn, *Random Rhymes frae Cullybackey* (Belfast: Baird, 1911).

32. [J.A. Todd (ed.)] *Livin' in Drumlister: the Collected Ballads of W.F. Marshall, 'The Bard of Tyrone'* (Belfast: Blackstaff Press, 1983) pp. 32-33.

33. Reviews are cited from 'Opinions of the Press' in Herbison, *Select Works*, pp. 313-326.

34. Thomas Beggs, *The Second Part of the Minstrel's Offering* (Belfast: Clark, 1836) p. [3].

35. Robert Huddleston, cited in *Ullans*, no. 1, Spring 1993, p. 11.

36. See the comments on the Rhyming Weavers in O'Donoghue, *The Poets of Ireland*; D.S. Crone, *A Concise Dictionary of Irish Biography* (Dublin: Talbot Press, 1928).

37. Hewitt, *Rhyming Weavers*, pp. 4-6.

38. John Hewitt, *Ulster Poets, 1800-1850* (Belfast: privately printed, 1951) p. 17.

39. For example, John Cooke (ed.), *The Dublin book of Irish Verse, 1728-1909* (Dublin: Hodges, Figgis, 1909).

40. Seamus Deane, *A Short History of Irish Literature* (London: Hutchinson, 1986).

41. ibid, p. 8.

42. Norman Vance, *Irish Literature: A Social History: Tradition, Identity and Difference* (Oxford: Blackwell, 1990) mentions David Herbison (pp. 127-128) and Francis Davis, 'The Belfast Man', (pp. 132-34). There is a short entry on 'weaver poets' in Robert Welch (ed.), *The Oxford Companion to Irish Literature*

(Oxford: Clarendon Press, 1996), which contains some inaccuracies.
43. Seamus Deane (ed.), *The Field Day Anthology of Irish Writing*. 3 vols (Derry: Field Day Publications, 1991).
44. Deane (ed.), *The Field Day Anthology of Irish Writing*, publisher's statement.
45. See, Bill Ashcroft, Gareth Griffiths and Helen Tiffin, *The Empire Writes Back: Theory and Practice in Post-Colonial Literatures* (London: Routledge, 1989).
46. Damian Smyth, 'Totalising imperative' [Review of *The Field Day Anthology of Irish Writing*], *Fortnight*, no. 309, September 1992, pp. 26-27.
47. 'View from the Linen Hall', *Linen Hall Review*, vol. 9, no. 2, Autumn 1992, p. 3.
48. Deane (ed.), *The Field Day Anthology of Irish Writing*, vol. 1, pp. 488-490.
49. Caroline Macafee (ed.), *A Concise Ulster Dictionary* (Oxford: Oxford University Press, 1996).
50. James Fenton, *The Hamely Tongue: A Personal Record of Ulster-Scots in County Antrim* (Newtownards: Ulster-Scots Academic Press, 1995).

INDEX